Spellex®

thesaurus

CURRICULUM ASSOCIATES®, Inc.

ISBN 1-55915-761-5

©2001, 1995—Curriculum Associates, Inc.
North Billerica, MA 01862

15 14 13 12 11 10 9 8 7 6 5 4 3 2

How to Use This Book

SPELLEX® Thesaurus is a book of common writing words and their synonyms. It is a useful writing tool. Go to the **SPELLEX**® Thesaurus when you want to replace a word with a different word or a word with a more precise meaning. When you avoid using the same words over and over, you improve your writing.

SPELLEX® Thesaurus contains over 1,200 entries. Each entry word is printed in bold type. All entry words are listed alphabetically. Beside each entry word is the part of speech. The part of speech tells whether the word is being used as a noun *(n)*, verb *(v)*, adjective *(adj)*, adverb *(adv)*, conjunction *(conj)*, or preposition *(prep)*. Synonyms for the entry word are given next. The synonyms, listed in alphabetical order, have an identical or a very similar meaning to the entry word. Last, the entry includes a sentence that uses the entry word in context. This sentence makes clear the meaning intended for the entry word and the synonyms listed. Here is an example of a **SPELLEX**® Thesaurus entry with all its parts:

hurt *(v)* ache, burn, pain, smart, sting

Does it <u>hurt</u> where you cut your finger?

The simple design of the **SPELLEX**® Thesaurus makes it easy to use. You can quickly search for synonyms that will make your stories, letters, and reports more lively and precise.

a

abandon (v) desert, forsake, leave

The sailors will abandon the sinking ship in a lifeboat.

able (adj) capable, competent, qualified, skilled

The pilot was able to land the plane safely.

about (adv) approximately, nearly, roughly

About 40,000 fans filled the football stadium.

absent (adj) away, gone, missing, omitted

Many students were absent from school because they had the flu.

absurd (adj) crazy, foolish, ridiculous, silly, wacky

Whoever had the absurd idea to ride over Niagara Falls in a barrel?

accept (v) admit, receive, welcome

Many restaurants accept credit cards to pay for meals.

accomplishment (n) achievement, attainment, effort, feat

Winning an Olympic gold medal is quite an accomplishment.

account (n) chronicle, narrative, report, story, tale

Grandpa's account of working in the circus was really funny.

accurate (adj) correct, exact, precise, right, true

Make sure your measurements are accurate before you cut the wood.

ache (v) hurt, suffer, throb

The secretary's fingers ache from typing all day.

acknowledge (v) admit, allow, concede, grant

I acknowledge that I make mistakes once in a while.

acquire (v) gain, get, obtain, win

The book collector will acquire enough rare books to fill three shelves.

act (v) do, perform, portray, represent

Will everyone in the class act in the school play?

action (n) accomplishment, act, deed, endeavor, feat

The firefighters' quick action put out the house fire.

active (adj) energetic, lively, spirited

Our puppy is active ali day long.

administration (n) command, government, management, organization

Many people are responsible for the administration of the federal government.

admire (v) esteem, honor, regard, respect, revere

I admire athletes who are really good at their sports.

admit (v) accept, receive, welcome

The usher will admit us to the theater after we show her our tickets.

adventure (n) enterprise, exploit, feat, venture

Lewis and Clark had a great adventure exploring the West in the early 1800s.

advertise (v) promote, publicize, push

The food company will advertise a new cereal on television and in magazines.

advise (v) counsel, recommend, suggest

Hotels advise their guests to lock valuable items in a safe.

affection (n) adoration, devotion, fondness, love, regard

The boys have real <u>affection</u> for their grandparents.

afraid (adj) apprehensive, fearful, frightened, scared, terrified

On Halloween, small children are sometimes <u>afraid</u> of other kids in costumes.

aged (adj) advanced, elderly, old, oldish

The <u>aged</u> couple have been married fifty years.

agreement (n) arrangement, contract, deal, pact, understanding

Management and labor drew up an <u>agreement</u> to work together.

aid (n) assistance, comfort, help, relief, support

We sent <u>aid</u> to the flood victims after they lost their homes.

aim (v) direct, head, point

<u>Aim</u> the arrow carefully before you let it go.

airy (adj) blowy, breezy, drafty, windy

We sat in an <u>airy</u> room looking out onto the ocean.

alarm (v) distress, frighten, scare, startle, terrify

Do strange noises <u>alarm</u> you at night?

alike (adj) comparable, corresponding, equivalent, like, similar

The twin boys look exactly <u>alike</u>.

all (adj) complete, entire, total, whole

<u>All</u> the planets revolve around the sun.

allow (v) authorize, let, permit, sanction

The town will <u>allow</u> us to skate on the pond when the ice gets thick enough.

almost (adv) about, approximately, nearly, practically, roughly

A softball is <u>almost</u> as big as a grapefruit.

alone (adj) apart, detached, isolated, separate, solitary

The shipwrecked sailor was <u>alone</u> on the desert island.

already (adv) before, earlier, formerly, once, previously

Haven't we <u>already</u> seen this episode of the television show?

also (adv) additionally, besides, furthermore, likewise, too

My cousin <u>also</u> goes to the same school I do.

although (conj) though, whereas, while

Sometimes both the sun and the moon appear in the sky, <u>although</u> only the moon appears at night.

altogether (adv) completely, entirely, fully, thoroughly, wholly

How many pieces of pie did you eat <u>altogether</u>?

amusing (adj) comical, funny, humorous, witty

We laughed at the <u>amusing</u> cartoon in the newspaper.

analyze (v) examine, inspect, investigate, scrutinize, study

Detectives <u>analyze</u> clues they collect at a crime scene.

anchor (v) catch, fasten, fix, moor, secure

Long steel wires <u>anchor</u> the television-antenna towers to the ground.

ancient (adj) aged, antique, old

This <u>ancient</u> castle is eight hundred years old.

angry *(adj)* enraged, furious, incensed, mad, vexed

I got really <u>angry</u> when my friends teased me about my haircut.

animated *(adj)* bright, lively, peppy, spirited, sprightly

My baby brother gets <u>animated</u> every time he goes to the zoo.

announce *(v)* broadcast, declare, proclaim, pronounce, state

The school principal will <u>announce</u> over the intercom the special events for that day.

answer *(n)* explanation, reply, response, retort

Does anyone know the <u>answer</u> to that question?

anticipate *(v)* envision, foresee, predict, prophesy

The weather forecaster doesn't <u>anticipate</u> any rain for the next few days.

anxious *(adj)* disturbed, nervous, troubled, uneasy, worried

The girl became <u>anxious</u> when her mother was an hour late picking her up in town.

apart *(adj)* detached, disconnected, separated

The doghouse sits <u>apart</u> from anything else in our backyard.

appear *(v)* emerge, loom, materialize, show

Wait for the moon to <u>appear</u> from behind the cloud.

apply *(v)* address, dedicate, devote, direct, focus

You must <u>apply</u> yourself to practicing the piano if you want to play well.

appointment *(n)* date, engagement, meeting, rendezvous

What time is your dental <u>appointment</u>?

appreciation *(n)* acknowledgment, gratefulness, gratitude, thankfulness, thanks

Call your grandparents to show them your <u>appreciation</u> for the presents they sent you.

approaching *(adj)* coming, imminent, impending, near

The people in the lifeboat cheered when they saw an <u>approaching</u> plane.

approve *(v)* accept, commend, favor, support, value

I hope my parents <u>approve</u> of my grades this term.

area *(n)* district, region, section, territory, zone

Our family lives in the <u>area</u> of the city near the airport.

argument *(n)* disagreement, dispute, fight, quarrel, spat

The sisters had an <u>argument</u> over which TV show to watch.

arrange *(v)* classify, group, order, organize, sort

Tomorrow I will <u>arrange</u> my CD collection alphabetically.

arrest *(v)* apprehend, bust, capture, nab, seize

Did the police officer <u>arrest</u> the thieves as they left the bank?

arrive *(v)* appear, come, enter, reach, show

My cousins will <u>arrive</u> here by train tonight.

article *(n)* composition, essay, paper, theme

When will the <u>article</u> you wrote appear in the local newspaper?

artificial *(adj)* fake, imitation, manufactured, mock, synthetic

If we had <u>artificial</u> grass in our yard, we would never have to mow.

ask (v) examine, inquire, interrogate, question, quiz

Stop at the gas station and <u>ask</u> for directions.

asleep (adj) dozing, sleeping, slumbering, snoozing

Were you still <u>asleep</u> in bed when the alarm went off?

assembly (n) crowd, gathering, group, mob, throng

The <u>assembly</u> in the town hall listened to the mayor's speech.

assist (v) aid, back, help, support

Nurses <u>assist</u> doctors during operations.

astonish (v) amaze, astound, awe, dazzle, surprise

As they swing from the trapeze, the circus acrobats <u>astonish</u> the crowd.

attack (v) assault, charge, raid, storm, strike

The soldiers will <u>attack</u> the enemy forces at night.

attempt (v) endeavor, strive, struggle, try, undertake

Watch the clown <u>attempt</u> to juggle three balls.

attend (v) mind, tend, watch

Please <u>attend</u> to the baby while I cook dinner.

attractive (adj) beautiful, gorgeous, handsome, lovely, pretty

A smile can make you look more <u>attractive</u>.

authority (n) command, control, mastery, might, power

Police have the <u>authority</u> to stop traffic if necessary.

automatic (adj) instinctive, involuntary, reflex, spontaneous

Blushing is an <u>automatic</u> response to being embarrassed.

available (adj) accessible, attainable, convenient, obtainable

We parked our car in the only space that was <u>available</u>.

average (adj) common, ordinary, typical, unexceptional, usual

An <u>average</u> winter day is usually cold.

avoid (v) bypass, dodge, duck, elude, evade

Try to <u>avoid</u> driving in rush-hour traffic.

awake (v) arise, awaken, rouse, stir, wake

Do you <u>awake</u> every morning wishing you could sleep some more?

awe (n) admiration, respect, reverence, wonder

The spectators were in <u>awe</u> of the gymnasts' performances.

awful (adj) appalling, dreadful, horrible, shocking, terrible

There were many <u>awful</u> creatures in the horror movie we saw last night.

awkward (adj) bumbling, clumsy, gawky, ungainly, ungraceful

The first time I wore roller blades, I looked very <u>awkward</u> trying to move.

b

babyish (adj) childish, immature, infantile, juvenile

Throwing a temper tantrum is <u>babyish</u> behavior.

bad (adj) evil, sinister, vicious, wicked

The big <u>bad</u> wolf went looking for a pig to eat.

badge (n) decoration, emblem, insignia, medal, medallion

The boy scout wore a <u>badge</u> on his shoulder.

bait (v) badger, harass, needle, taunt, tease

Do you ever <u>bait</u> your brother to make him mad?

bake (v) broil, cook, roast

Put the bread in the oven to <u>bake</u>.

band (n) crew, gang, group, party, ring

A <u>band</u> of thieves robbed the neighborhood.

bang (n) blast, boom, crack, crash, explosion

The race began with a <u>bang</u> from the starter's pistol.

bar (v) block, hamper, hinder, restrain, stop

Police barriers <u>bar</u> the parade crowd from the street.

bare (adj) exposed, naked, nude, unclad, undressed

When I got out of the bath, my <u>bare</u> skin got cold.

bargain (n) agreement, arrangement, contract, deal, pact

I made a <u>bargain</u> to trade my baseball glove for a soccer ball.

basic (adj) elementary, essential, fundamental, primary

Fruits are one of the <u>basic</u> food groups.

bat (v) hit, rap, strike, swat, whack

<u>Bat</u> the ball against the wall.

bathe (v) douse, immerse, shower, soak, wash

Do you <u>bathe</u> yourself every day?

battle (n) clash, combat, conflict, fight, struggle

Many soldiers died fighting in the <u>battle</u>.

beam (v) blaze, glow, illuminate, radiate, shine

The searchlights <u>beam</u> across the dark sky.

bear (v) carry, shoulder, support, sustain, uphold

The building's foundation can <u>bear</u> a fifty-floor skyscraper.

beast (n) brute, fiend, ghoul, monster, savage

Only a terrible <u>beast</u> would harm others.

beat (v) batter, hammer, hit, pelt, pound

The drummers <u>beat</u> their instruments loudly.

beautiful (adj) attractive, gorgeous, handsome, lovely, pretty

What a <u>beautiful</u> baby!

becoming (adj) attractive, flattering, pleasing

The color red is quite <u>becoming</u> on you.

before (adv) already, earlier, formerly, previously, sooner

Had you ever seen a solar eclipse <u>before</u>?

beg (v) appeal, ask, beseech, implore, plead

We always <u>beg</u> the baby-sitter to let us stay up later.

begin (v) commence, initiate, launch, start, undertake

<u>Begin</u> taking the test now.

behavior (n) actions, bearing, conduct, manner, way

Your <u>behavior</u> could use some improvement.

belief (n) conviction, feeling, notion, opinion, view

His belief that he can win the contest gives him confidence.

bend (n) angle, bow, curve, turn, twist

The river has a bend in it just before the waterfall.

benefit (n) advantage, good, gain, profit

What is the benefit of putting my savings into a bank account?

besides (adv) also, anyway, additionally, furthermore, moreover

Apples are healthful to eat; besides, they taste good.

best (adj) finest, greatest, premium, superior, superlative

What is the best ice cream you've ever tasted?

bet (v) chance, gamble, risk, stake, wager

I bet you can't jump as high as a kangaroo.

big (adj) enormous, gigantic, huge, immense, large

An elephant is a big animal.

bill (n) account, invoice, statement, tab

Was the restaurant bill larger than you had expected?

bind (v) fasten, knot, secure, tie

Bind the rope tightly.

birth (n) beginning, commencement, origin, start

Every Fourth of July, we celebrate the birth of our nation.

bite (v) chew, chomp, gnaw, munch, nibble

Bite carefully so you don't hurt your teeth.

black (adj) ebony, inky, jet

The black cat was hard to see at night.

blame (v) accuse, condemn, criticize, fault, reproach

Who's to blame for making this mess?

blast (n) bang, boom, discharge, eruption, explosion

The blast at the mine sounded like thunder.

blaze (n) burning, combustion, fire, flame

The firefighters could barely contain the blaze.

bloom (v) blossom, bud, flower

Plants bloom in the spring.

blow (n) crack, strike, swat, thump, whack

The boxer took a great blow on the chin.

bluff (v) deceive, fool, mislead, trick

Do you like to bluff during card games?

boil (v) bubble, seethe, simmer, stew

How long will it take for the pot of water on the stove to boil?

bond (n) attachment, connection, link, tie

The new friends made a strong bond during their weeks at camp.

bony (adj) gaunt, lean, scrawny, skinny, thin

Her clothes fit loosely on her bony frame.

border (n) edge, fringe, margin, perimeter, rim

The gardener planted flowers around the border of the yard.

boring (adj) dreary, dull, tedious, tiresome, uninteresting

It's boring to hear the same thing over and over again.

boss (n) chief, director, head, leader, manager

The factory workers like their boss because she treats them fairly.

bother (v) annoy, bug, disturb, irritate, pester

Don't bother me when I'm studying!

bottom (n) base, sole, underneath, underside

The bottom of my shoes got very muddy.

bound (v) hop, jump, leap, spring, vault

The hikers will bound from one rock to another to cross the stream.

bow (v) bend, hump, hunch, scrunch, stoop

The knight must bow to his queen.

boy (n) chap, fellow, lad

A boy will grow up to be a man.

brain (n) intellect, intelligence, mind, reason, understanding

Use your brain to solve the crossword puzzle.

branch (n) arm, bough, limb

Cut the dead branch from that old oak tree.

brave (adj) courageous, fearless, gallant, heroic, valiant

I feel brave when I do a back flip off the diving board.

break (v) fracture, shatter, smash, splinter

Who threw the rock that made the window break?

breezy (adj) airy, blowy, gusty, windy

It was breezy on the beach and our umbrella blew over.

brief (adj) fleeting, momentary, short, temporary

For a brief time, a rainbow appeared in the sky.

bright (adj) alert, brilliant, clever, intelligent, smart

The bright student won a math award.

brilliant (adj) bright, dazzling, luminous, radiant, shining

The diamond necklace was brilliant.

bring (v) bear, carry, convey, deliver, transport

Bring the ball over here so we can start the game.

brisk (adj) energetic, lively, quick, sprightly, vigorous

On walks, do you like to stroll or to move at a brisk pace?

broad (adj) ample, expansive, extensive, spacious, wide

The broad street had room for parking on both sides.

brush (v) flick, glance, graze, skim, touch

Did you brush against the chalkboard to get those white streaks on your clothes?

bug (n) defect, fault, flaw, imperfection, problem

The computer software program has a bug in it.

build (v) construct, erect, raise, rear

Carpenters can build a house in a few weeks.

bump (n) bulge, knot, lump, swelling

There's a bump on my arm where the baseball hit it.

bunch (n) batch, bundle, clump, cluster, group

Here's a bunch of grapes to eat.

bundle (n) package, packet, parcel

How much will it cost to mail that big bundle?

burden (n) affliction, cross, hardship, ordeal, trial

Being jobless was a real burden to the couple.

burn (v) blaze, combust, flame, flare, ignite
Dry kindling will burn very quickly.

burst (v) blast, explode, pop
The fireworks will burst in the night sky.

busy (adj) active, bustling, energetic, lively, vigorous
Do you feel as busy as a beaver?

but (conj) except, however, only, yet
I like rock music, but I also like jazz.

buy (n) bargain, deal, steal, value
That portable cassette player is a great buy!

bypass (v) avoid, dodge, duck, sidestep, skirt
These roads bypass the downtown part of the city.

C

cage (v) coop, enclose, envelop, fence, pen
Most zoos cage their lions.

call (v) cry, holler, shout, yell
Call to me when you're ready to leave.

calm (adj) collected, composed, placid, serene, tranquil
Are you able to stay calm before a test?

campaign (n) crusade, drive, push
Were you active in the mayor's political campaign?

cane (n) pole, rod, staff, stick
The elderly man walks with a cane.

cap (n) plug, seal, stopper, top
Put the cap on the soda bottle.

capable (adj) able, competent, qualified, skilled
The pitcher is capable of getting the batter out.

capacity (n) ability, capability, competence, potential, qualification
I have the capacity to do well at my new job.

capital (n) assets, means, resources, wealth
Do you have enough capital to invest in the new business?

capture (v) apprehend, arrest, catch, nab, seize
Have the police been able to capture the thief?

care (n) carefulness, caution, concern, heedfulness, regard
Always take care around wild animals.

carry (v) bear, convey, haul, lug, transport
Do you carry your lunch in a sack or lunch box?

case (n) example, illustration, instance, sample, specimen
It's a case of love at first sight.

cash (n) currency, dollars, greenbacks, loot, money
Banks have lots of cash in their vaults.

cast (v) hurl, pitch, sling, throw, toss
The hiker cast aside his empty canteen in the desert.

catalog (v) inventory, list, log, record, tally
It will take weeks to catalog everything in the warehouse.

catch (v) grab, grasp, nab, seize, snatch
The left fielder can catch every ball hit to her.

choose

cause (v) effect, generate, induce, make, produce

Too much sun on your skin can <u>cause</u> sunburn.

caution (n) care, carefulness, heedfulness, wariness

Use <u>caution</u> when crossing a busy street.

celebration (n) festival, festivity, holiday, party, revelry

The Fourth of July <u>celebration</u> ended with fireworks.

center (n) core, middle, midpoint, midst

The <u>center</u> of the earth is molten metal.

certain (adj) confident, convinced, definite, positive, sure

Gamblers are always <u>certain</u> they will win.

certify (v) testify, verify, vouch

Can you <u>certify</u> that you live at the address given?

chain (n) sequence, series, string, succession, train

What <u>chain</u> of events led to your accident?

chance (n) likelihood, odds, possibility, probability

There was only a small <u>chance</u> I would win the race.

change (v) alter, convert, modify, vary

A caterpillar will <u>change</u> into a butterfly.

channel (n) canal, course, waterway

This <u>channel</u> carries water from the river.

character (n) honesty, honor, principles, reputation

The judge's <u>character</u> is admirable.

charge (n) care, custody, guardianship, supervision, trust

A baby-sitter was put in <u>charge</u> of the children.

charity (n) compassion, generosity, goodwill, kindness

Do you show <u>charity</u> to people less fortunate than yourself?

charm (v) bewitch, enchant, fascinate

Don't try to <u>charm</u> me with flattery.

chase (v) follow, hunt, pursue, track, trail

Is it true that dogs like to <u>chase</u> cats?

cheap (adj) inexpensive, low-cost, low-priced, reasonable

If you buy a <u>cheap</u> watch, it might break.

check (v) examine, inspect, scrutinize, study, survey

The inspectors <u>check</u> the goods for flaws.

cheerful (adj) bright, happy, lighthearted, merry

The <u>cheerful</u> campers sang as they hiked through the woods.

chew (v) chomp, crunch, gnaw, munch, nibble

<u>Chew</u> your food well before swallowing.

chief (n) boss, director, head, leader, master

The construction <u>chief</u> told her workers what to do.

child (n) juvenile, kid, youngster, youth

A <u>child</u> needs more food than a baby does.

chilly (adj) cold, cool, nippy

It's <u>chilly</u> on many days in the winter and late fall.

choose (v) pick, select, take

If you could <u>choose</u> one wish, what would it be?

13

chop (v) cut, fell, hack, whack

The lumberjack will use an ax to <u>chop</u> the wood.

circle (v) orbit, revolve, rotate, turn

The space shuttle will <u>circle</u> the earth and return in seven days.

circulate (v) disperse, distribute, spread

How did the news <u>circulate</u> so quickly?

civil (adj) courteous, mannerly, polite, refined, well-mannered

Store clerks should always be <u>civil</u> to their customers.

claim (v) allege, assert, declare, maintain, state

Those strangers <u>claim</u> to be my relatives.

class (n) category, classification, grade, group, rank

What <u>class</u> will you be in next year?

clean (adj) immaculate, spotless, stainless, unsoiled

Take your <u>clean</u> clothes out of the washing machine.

clear (adj) bright, cloudless, fair, fine, sunny

A <u>clear</u> sky is blue.

clever (adj) alert, bright, intelligent, sharp, smart

That was a <u>clever</u> remark.

climate (n) atmosphere, environment, surroundings

A tropical <u>climate</u> can be very humid.

climb (v) ascend, mount, scale

Can we <u>climb</u> this mountain without much gear?

cloak (n) cape, coat, garment, robe, wrap

The heavy <u>cloak</u> kept the traveler warm.

close (adj) immediate, near, nearby

We live <u>close</u> to the library and go there often.

close (v) bolt, fasten, latch, lock, shut

<u>Close</u> the door behind you.

clothes (n) attire, clothing, dress, garments

People wear more <u>clothes</u> in the winter than the summer.

cloudy (adj) foggy, hazy, misty, overcast, unclear

The sky looks <u>cloudy</u> when it rains.

clown (n) fool, humorist, jester, joker

The circus <u>clown</u> made everyone laugh.

club (n) association, league, organization, society, union

Members of the hiking <u>club</u> meet once a month.

coarse (adj) grainy, gritty, rough

This sandpaper is <u>coarse</u>.

cold (adj) chilly, cool, freezing, frigid, nippy

When it's <u>cold</u>, you can see your breath.

collect (v) accumulate, amass, pile, raise

Many people <u>collect</u> old coins as their hobby.

colony (n) dependency, possession, province, territory

Australia is a former <u>colony</u> of Great Britain.

color (n) hue, shade, tint, tone

What <u>color</u> do you want to paint the house?

column (n) pillar, post, shaft, support

A building needs more than one <u>column</u> to hold up the roof.

come (v) appear, arrive, reach, show

Please <u>come</u> home with me after school.

comfort (v) cheer, console, pacify, soothe

The parents <u>comfort</u> their child when he is sad.

command (v) bid, charge, direct, instruct, order

I wish I could <u>command</u> a robot to clean my room.

commence (v) arise, begin, originate, start

The race is about to <u>commence</u>.

common (adj) everyday, familiar, frequent, regular, routine

Will a cure ever be found for the <u>common</u> cold?

communicate (v) convey, disclose, spread, tell, transmit

I <u>communicate</u> with my grandparents by phone.

companion (n) buddy, chum, friend, mate, pal

Will a <u>companion</u> accompany you on your trip?

company (n) business, corporation, enterprise, establishment, firm

My uncle works for a <u>company</u> that makes widgets.

complete (adj) entire, full, intact, total, whole

My collection of baseball cards is almost <u>complete</u>.

composed (adj) calm, collected, placid, serene, tranquil

The basketball players tried to stay <u>composed</u> before the big game.

conclude (v) cease, close, end, finish, terminate

When will the business meeting <u>conclude</u>?

condition (n) situation, state, status

The patient's <u>condition</u> improved from serious to stable.

conduct (v) direct, manage, operate, run, supervise

Most professors <u>conduct</u> their classes from the front of the room.

confer (v) award, bestow, give, grant, present

Does the college <u>confer</u> scholarships to needy students?

confine (v) bar, limit, restrict

We usually <u>confine</u> our hamster to its cage.

confirm (v) authenticate, justify, verify

Can anyone <u>confirm</u> that your statement is true?

conform (v) adapt, adjust, fit

Do you easily <u>conform</u> to new situations?

confuse (v) baffle, bewilder, confound, perplex, puzzle

Don't ask too many questions, or you'll <u>confuse</u> me.

connect (v) couple, join, link, tie, unite

Help me <u>connect</u> the train tracks together.

conquer (v) beat, defeat, overcome, overpower, subdue

Did the Vikings ever <u>conquer</u> the Huns?

consent (n) approval, authorization, permission

You'll need your parents' <u>consent</u> to go on the field trip.

consider (v) contemplate, ponder, study, weigh

Will the graduate <u>consider</u> a future in computers?

constant (adj) consistent, invariable, same, unchanging

The ebb and flow of the ocean waves is <u>constant</u>.

construct *(v)* assemble, build, erect, make, raise

Did you <u>construct</u> this dinosaur model?

content *(adj)* fulfilled, gratified, happy, satisfied

After playing hockey all morning, I was <u>content</u> to watch in the afternoon.

contest *(n)* competition, game, meet, match

Whoever shoots the most bull's-eyes will win the archery <u>contest</u>.

continue *(v)* recommence, renew, reopen, restart, resume

Does this article <u>continue</u> on the next page?

control *(v)* direct, dominate, govern, lead, manage

Who will <u>control</u> the company now that it has been sold?

convene *(v)* assemble, collect, congregate, gather, meet

The meeting will <u>convene</u> at eight o'clock.

convenient *(adj)* accessible, adjacent, available, handy, nearby

Our apartment is <u>convenient</u> to the school.

conversation *(n)* chat, communication, dialogue, discussion, talking

What was the topic of your <u>conversation</u>?

cool *(adj)* calm, collected, composed, nonchalant, serene

The track star stayed <u>cool</u> under pressure.

cooperate *(v)* band, league, unite

If we <u>cooperate</u>, we'll get the job done quicker.

copy *(v)* duplicate, imitate, reproduce

This machine can <u>copy</u> your picture.

correct *(adj)* accurate, exact, precise, right, true

Were all your answers <u>correct</u>?

cost *(n)* charge, expense, price

The discount store sells items at a lower <u>cost</u>.

costume *(n)* clothes, clothing, dress, guise, outfit

The actor wore a special <u>costume</u> in the play.

count *(v)* calculate, compute, number, numerate, tally

How many people do you <u>count</u> in the audience?

courage *(n)* bravery, nerve, spirit, spunk, valor

It takes <u>courage</u> to admit mistakes.

court *(n)* courtyard, enclosure, yard

The <u>court</u> is in the middle of the castle.

cover *(v)* cloak, conceal, hide, screen, veil

No one will recognize you if you <u>cover</u> your face with a hood.

crack *(n)* break, chink, cleft, fracture, split

There was a <u>crack</u> in the ice.

crash *(n)* collision, impact, smash

The car <u>crash</u> tied up traffic for miles.

crawl *(v)* creep, slide, snake, worm

Babies <u>crawl</u> before they walk.

crazy *(adj)* absurd, foolish, ridiculous, silly, wacky

Wearing a Halloween costume to the Valentine's Day party was a <u>crazy</u> idea.

create *(v)* compose, form, make, produce

Use this clay to <u>create</u> a sculpture.

crime *(n)* felony, misdeed, offense, violation

Robbing banks is a <u>crime</u>.

cross (adj) crabby, cranky, grouchy, irritable, testy

The supermarket customers were <u>cross</u> from standing in the checkout line so long.

crouch (v) huddle, hunch, stoop

Don't <u>crouch</u> down in your seat.

crowd (n) flock, gathering, mob, throng

The baseball game drew a large <u>crowd</u>.

crush (v) compress, mash, press, squash, squish

A cider press will <u>crush</u> apples into cider.

cry (v) bawl, blubber, sob, wail, weep

Babies <u>cry</u> a lot.

cultivate (v) foster, nourish, nurse

Do you know how to <u>cultivate</u> a garden?

cunning (adj) crafty, foxy, sly, tricky

The <u>cunning</u> fox tricked the gingerbread boy.

curious (adj) inquisitive, investigative, questioning, wondering

I asked the question because I was <u>curious</u>.

current (adj) contemporary, immediate, ongoing, present

We study <u>current</u> events in school.

curve (n) arc, bow, crook, round, turn

Watch out for a sudden <u>curve</u> in the road.

custom (n) habit, manner, practice, way

It's our <u>custom</u> to eat turkey on Thanksgiving.

cut (v) gash, pierce, slash, slice, slit

Did you <u>cut</u> your knee when you fell on the pavement?

d

dad (n) daddy, father, pa, papa, pop

My <u>dad</u> looks like me, only bigger.

damage (n) breakage, destruction, wreckage

The <u>damage</u> from the hurricane was tremendous.

danger (n) hazard, peril, risk

Is there any <u>danger</u> of coming upon a grizzly bear in these woods?

daring (adj) adventurous, bold, fearless, hardy, venturesome

The trapeze artist was <u>daring</u>.

dark (adj) dim, dusky, gloomy, shadowy

It was <u>dark</u> in the woods at night.

darling (n) beloved, dear, honey, sweetheart

I love you, <u>darling</u>.

dash (v) hurry, race, rush, whiz, zip

Let's <u>dash</u> to the store before it closes.

dawn (n) daybreak, daylight, morning, sunrise, sunup

Why do roosters crow at <u>dawn</u>?

dead (adj) deceased, extinct, late, lifeless, perished

The <u>dead</u> plant never got enough water.

deal (n) agreement, arrangement, contract, pact, understanding

We made a <u>deal</u> to buy a new car.

deceive (v) betray, double-cross, fool, mislead, trick

Magicians try to <u>deceive</u> their audience.

decide (v) conclude, determine, resolve, settle

Will a judge <u>decide</u> the case in court?

declare (v) advertise, announce, broadcast, proclaim

Soon the disc jockey will declare the winner of the radio contest.

decline (v) dismiss, refuse, reject, spurn

Why did you decline their kind offer of help?

defeat (v) beat, conquer, overcome, overpower, subdue

In a war, one country tries to defeat another.

defend (v) guard, protect, safeguard, secure, shield

The knights will defend the castle from attack.

delicate (adj) dainty, elegant, fine, refined

The spider's web was shiny and delicate.

delicious (adj) appetizing, flavorful, savory, tasty

That was a delicious meal!

delighted (adj) ecstatic, excited, glad, happy, pleased

We were delighted with our seats for the play.

deliver (v) dispense, furnish, give, provide, supply

The postal carrier will deliver the mail.

depart (v) exit, go, leave, quit, withdraw

The circus will depart after the last show.

describe (v) narrate, recite, recount, relate, report

Let me describe where we went on vacation.

desert (v) abandon, forsake, leave

A captain must never desert a sinking ship.

desire (n) craving, longing, urge, yearning

Do you have any desire to eat tacos for dinner?

despair (n) desperation, hopelessness, melancholy, misery, sadness

The townspeople felt despair after the tornado destroyed their property.

destroy (v) demolish, destruct, ruin, smash, wreck

The iceberg could destroy the ship if they collide.

determine (v) conclude, decide, resolve, settle

How did the detectives determine who committed the crime?

develop (v) age, grow, mature, ripen

Someday that sapling will develop into a tall tree.

die (v) decease, depart, perish

The crops will die if it doesn't rain soon.

different (adj) dissimilar, diverse, unlike, unsimilar

The twins are very different from each other even though they look the same.

difficult (adj) hard, laborious, strenuous, tough

Climbing to the top of the mountain was difficult.

dig (v) excavate, scoop, shovel

We hope to dig up some dinosaur fossils.

dim (adj) dark, dusky, gloomy, obscure, shadowy

The light was dim in the cave.

dip (v) douse, duck, dunk, immerse, submerge

Dip your foot into the pool to test the water.

direct (v) control, govern, lead, manage, run

Who will direct the company when the president retires?

dirty *(adj)* filthy, grimy, grubby, soiled, unclean

The pigs were <u>dirty</u> after playing in the mud.

disappear *(v)* evaporate, fade, vanish

Use this cream to make your rash <u>disappear</u>.

discover *(v)* ascertain, determine, find, learn, unearth

Explorers <u>discover</u> new places to go.

discuss *(v)* argue, debate, deliberate, dispute, talk

Let's <u>discuss</u> the situation over dinner.

disgraceful *(adj)* dishonorable, shabby, shameful

The way the king treated his servants was <u>disgraceful</u>.

dismiss *(v)* discharge, drop, fire, sack, terminate

My boss will <u>dismiss</u> me from my job if I mess up again.

displeasing *(adj)* disagreeable, offensive, unpleasant

The smell from the paper mill was <u>displeasing</u>.

dispose *(v)* discard, ditch, dump, eliminate, junk

Please <u>dispose</u> of the trash at the dump.

dispute *(n)* argument, disagreement, fight, quarrel

The tenants had a <u>dispute</u> with their landlord.

distant *(adj)* far, faraway, far-off, remote, removed

The <u>distant</u> sound of sirens got louder as the fire engines approached.

district *(n)* area, division, quarter, region, section

Most of the city's skyscrapers are clustered in the business <u>district</u>.

ditch *(v)* discard, dispose, dump, junk

I should <u>ditch</u> these ragged clothes.

dive *(v)* leap, lunge, plunge

Who will <u>dive</u> into the pool first?

divide *(v)* part, partition, section, segment, separate

<u>Divide</u> the pie into eight pieces.

do *(v)* accomplish, achieve, execute, perform

What will you <u>do</u> next?

double *(adj)* dual, duplicate, twofold

The couple needs a <u>double</u> stroller for their twins.

doubt *(v)* dispute, mistrust, question

My lawyer and I <u>doubt</u> you're telling the truth.

draft *(n)* outline, rough, skeleton, sketch, version

Will you write a quick <u>draft</u> of the proposal?

drag *(v)* haul, lug, pull, tow, tug

We had to <u>drag</u> my little sister through the museum.

dream *(n)* fancy, fantasy, illusion, nightmare, vision

A happy <u>dream</u> is better than a scary one.

dress *(n)* frock, gown, robe

My mother wore a fancy <u>dress</u> to the wedding.

drill *(n)* exercise, practice, rehearsal, training

The firefighters do a special <u>drill</u> every week.

drive

encouraging

drive (v) propel, push, shove, thrust

Use the hammer to <u>drive</u> the nail into the wood.

drop (v) decline, descend, dip, fall, sink

We like to catch snowflakes on our tongue as they <u>drop</u> from the sky.

dry (adj) arid, dehydrated, moistureless, parched

The <u>dry</u> desert air made the backpacker thirsty.

duck (v) avoid, dodge, evade, sidestep, skirt

The politician tried to <u>duck</u> a tricky question.

due (adj) anticipated, awaited, expected, scheduled

The children are not home from school yet, but they are <u>due</u> shortly.

dull (adj) boring, dreary, tedious, tiresome, uninteresting

The <u>dull</u> speech put me to sleep.

dumb (adj) inarticulate, mute, silent, speechless, voiceless

The sailor was struck <u>dumb</u> with joy at finally sighting land.

e

eager (adj) ardent, avid, excited, impatient, keen

The runners were <u>eager</u> for the road race to begin.

early (adv) ahead, beforehand, prematurely

The baseball game ended <u>early</u> due to a storm.

earn (v) acquire, gain, get, make, win

I <u>earn</u> money by mowing lawns.

easy (adj) effortless, simple, smooth, straightforward

Was it <u>easy</u> to reschedule your appointment?

eat (v) consume, devour, dine, feast, feed

Always <u>eat</u> a healthful breakfast.

edge (n) border, fringe, perimeter, rim

The <u>edge</u> of the cookies were burnt.

educate (v) instruct, school, teach, train, tutor

You can <u>educate</u> yourself by reading a lot.

effect (n) consequence, outcome, result

The bright sun had the <u>effect</u> of melting the snow.

effort (n) endeavor, exertion, struggle, trouble

Put some <u>effort</u> into your schoolwork.

elaborate (adj) complex, complicated, fancy, intricate, involved

The actors wore <u>elaborate</u> costumes.

elect (v) choose, pick, select

We <u>elect</u> a president every four years.

elevate (v) boost, heighten, hoist, lift, raise

The roofers will <u>elevate</u> their supplies with a rope and pulley.

empire (n) kingdom, monarchy, realm

The British built an <u>empire</u> that extended around the world.

empty (adj) bare, barren, unfilled, vacant, void

Throw this <u>empty</u> box into the trash.

encouraging (adj) cheering, hopeful, likely, promising, rosy

The good weather was an <u>encouraging</u> sign for the picnic.

end

exciting

end *(v)* cease, close, conclude, finish, terminate

What time in the afternoon does school end?

endure *(v)* abide, bear, suffer, sustain, tolerate

Some people can endure pain better than others.

enjoyable *(adj)* favorable, gratifying, pleasant, pleasing, pleasurable

Did you have an enjoyable time at the restaurant?

enormous *(adj)* colossal, gigantic, huge, immense, tremendous

King Kong was an enormous gorilla.

entertaining *(adj)* amusing, engaging, funny, interesting

A storyteller told us an entertaining tale.

entire *(adj)* complete, full, intact, total, whole

The entire cast of the play took a bow.

equipment *(n)* apparatus, gear, materials, stuff

Have you packed all your camp equipment?

erase *(v)* cancel, delete, eliminate, remove

Please erase all the words on the chalkboard.

erect *(v)* build, construct, raise, rear

There is a plan to erect a new skyscraper on the vacant city lot.

escape *(v)* bolt, flee, fly, skip

Do many prisoners try to escape from jail?

essay *(n)* article, composition, paper, theme

The student's essay was published in a magazine.

essential *(adj)* necessary, needed, required

This clue is essential to solving the riddle.

establish *(v)* install, place, set, settle

The settlers hoped to establish a town at the mouth of the river.

estimate *(v)* appraise, evaluate, rate, value

Can you estimate how much this antique is worth?

even *(adj)* flat, flush, level, smooth

The prairie looks even to the horizon.

event *(n)* episode, happening, incident, occasion, occurrence

What was the biggest sports event of the year?

evil *(adj)* bad, sinister, vicious, wicked

In fairy tales, evil characters usually pay their dues.

exact *(adj)* accurate, correct, precise

Do you have exact change for the toll?

examine *(v)* check, inspect, scrutinize, study, survey

Examine the evidence carefully.

example *(n)* case, illustration, instance, sample, specimen

Give me an example of what you mean.

excel *(v)* exceed, outdo, outshine, surpass

Someday I hope to excel at skating.

exceptional *(adj)* extraordinary, phenomenal, rare, remarkable, unique

The musician has exceptional talent.

exchange *(v)* change, substitute, swap, switch, trade

Can I exchange this shirt for one in a larger size?

exciting *(adj)* exhilarating, inspiring, rousing, stimulating, thrilling

The close score kept the game exciting.

excuse (n) alibi, defense, explanation, plea, reason

What's your excuse for being late?

execute (v) accomplish, achieve, do, perform

Will the skier execute a perfect jump?

exhibit (n) exhibition, fair, show

The museum exhibit filled three halls.

exist (v) be, breathe, live

We exist on the planet Earth.

expert (n) authority, master, pro, whiz, wizard

The black-belt wearer is an expert at karate.

explain (v) clarify, illustrate, interpret

Please explain this problem so that I will understand it.

explode (v) blast, burst, discharge, fire

The bomb was set to explode in five minutes.

explore (v) investigate, probe, scout, search

Scientists will explore the cause of the earthquake.

express (v) communicate, convey, declare, say, tell

Can you express how you're feeling?

extent (n) length, range, reach, span

Do you realize the extent of the damage?

extra (adj) added, additional, further, more, other

Wear an extra pair of socks to keep your feet warm.

extreme (adj) farthest, furthermost, furthest, outermost, remotest

The Arctic Circle is in the extreme north.

f

fade (v) disappear, disperse, evaporate, vanish

The sunburn will fade after a few days.

fair (adj) clear, cloudless, fine, sunny

The weather report predicts fair skies tomorrow.

fall (v) drop, pitch, plunge, topple, tumble

The books were about to fall from the library shelf.

false (adj) inaccurate, incorrect, untrue, wrong

Is the statement true or false.

fame (n) celebrity, famousness, renown, reputation

The actor gained fame from his first movie.

familiar (adj) chummy, close, friendly, intimate

Are you familiar with any of your neighbors?

family (n) clan, folk, lineage, relations, relatives

Our entire family gets together on holidays.

famous (adj) famed, noted, notorious, prominent, well-known

The famous author has written many best-sellers.

fancy (adj) complicated, elaborate, intricate, lavish

The birthday cake had fancy decorations on top.

far (adj) distant, faraway, far-off, remote, removed

That far cloud means a storm is coming.

fashion (n) craze, fad, style, trend

Will short skirts be this year's fashion for women?

fast *(adv)* hastily, quickly, rapidly, speedily, swiftly

Make up your mind fast.

fasten *(v)* affix, attach, connect, fix, secure

Fasten the lock on the door.

fat *(adj)* chubby, heavy, overweight, plump, stout

The fat clown rolled around the stage.

fault *(n)* blemish, defect, flaw, imperfection, shortcoming

His biggest fault is that he is always late.

favor *(n)* courtesy, kindness, service

Could you do me a small favor and water my plants while we're away?

favorite *(adj)* favored, popular, preferred, well-liked

The girl read her favorite book at least ten times.

fear *(n)* dread, fright, horror, panic, terror

Many small children have a fear of the dark.

feeble *(adj)* delicate, fragile, frail, weak

The sick horse was too feeble to stand up.

feed *(v)* consume, devour, dine, eat, feast

The pigs feed from the trough.

feel *(v)* finger, handle, touch

Feel how soft and silky the baby's skin is.

fierce *(adj)* cruel, ferocious, inhuman, savage, vicious

What would you do if you heard the fierce growl of a grizzly bear?

fight *(n)* brawl, fray, scuffle, tussle

The fight began when someone tried to cut in line.

figure *(v)* calculate, compute, estimate

Can you figure the sum in your head or do you need paper and pencil?

fill *(v)* block, clog, close, plug, stop

Use putty to fill in the hole.

final *(adj)* closing, concluding, last, latest, ultimate

The final score was a tie.

find *(v)* detect, locate, pinpoint, spot, uncover

Did the private investigator find any important clues?

fine *(adj)* dainty, delicate, elegant, exquisite

There is fine embroidery on that blouse.

finish *(v)* close, complete, conclude, end, terminate

Finish dinner before eating dessert.

firm *(adj)* determined, tough, unbending, unyielding

The school has very firm rules.

first *(adj)* earliest, initial, original, primary

The first ship to circle the world was Magellan's.

fit *(adj)* appropriate, apt, fitting, proper, suitable

The villain of the play gets a fit punishment.

fix *(v)* mend, patch, repair, right

Can you fix the ripped jacket?

flash *(v)* gleam, glimmer, shimmer, sparkle, twinkle

The lighthouse beam will flash every few seconds.

flat *(adj)* even, flush, level, smooth

A stovepipe hat is flat on top.

flee *(v)* bolt, fly, run, scamper, scoot

The villagers must flee if the nearby volcano erupts.

flow (n) current, drift, flood, stream, tide

The flow of the river moves quickly downstream.

fly (v) flit, flutter, sail, soar, sweep

Many birds fly south in the winter.

follow (v) chase, pursue, track, trail

The bear will follow the bees back to their hive.

fond (adj) affectionate, devoted, loving

I am very fond of my best friend.

fool (v) deceive, delude, dupe, mislead, trick

Can the magician fool you with a trick?

forbid (v) ban, outlaw, prohibit

Our laws forbid murder and robbery.

force (v) compel, make, pressure

You can't force me to like spinach.

foreign (adj) alien, exotic, strange, unfamiliar

Do you speak any foreign languages?

forget (v) disregard, ignore, miss, neglect, overlook

Don't forget to lock the door.

form (v) model, mold, shape

The potter will form a vase from that lump of clay.

former (adj) past, preceding, previous, prior

The worker learned computer skills in his former job.

fortune (n) riches, treasure, wealth, worth

The pirates buried a fortune in treasure.

foul (adj) disgusting, nasty, repulsive, revolting, sickening

Is that foul smell coming from the town dump?

found (v) create, establish, institute, organize, start

The pioneers will found a new town in the wilderness.

fracture (n) breach, break, rupture, split

The earthquake caused a fracture in the highway.

fragrance (n) aroma, perfume, scent

The new fragrance smelled like roses.

frail (adj) delicate, feeble, fragile, weak

My great-grandmother is quite frail.

frank (adj) candid, direct, straightforward

Let's be frank about our disagreements.

free (v) discharge, liberate, release

Could you free the animal caught in the trap?

freezing (adj) cold, frigid, frosty, icy, wintry

Wear many layers of clothing in freezing weather.

freight (n) burden, cargo, haul, load

The train carries a lot of freight.

fresh (adj) innovative, inventive, new, novel, original

The politician needs fresh ideas for her campaign.

friend (n) buddy, chum, companion, pal, playmate

My best friend and I have a lot in common.

frighten (v) alarm, scare, startle, terrify, terrorize

Do horror movies frighten you?

frosty (adj) cold, freezing, frigid, icy, wintry

The windows looked frosty during the blizzard.

full *(adj)* crammed, jammed, loaded, packed, stuffed

The toy chest was too <u>full</u> to close tight.

funny *(adj)* amusing, comical, humorous, zany

I laughed out loud reading the <u>funny</u> story.

furious *(adj)* angry, enraged, incensed, mad

The tourist was <u>furious</u> when his car was stolen.

furnish *(v)* equip, gear, outfit, rig, supply

They will <u>furnish</u> their new apartment as soon as they save some money.

g

gain *(v)* acquire, get, obtain, win

What will you <u>gain</u> by cheating?

gang *(n)* band, crew, crowd, group, pack

The whole <u>gang</u> is here for the party.

gather *(v)* assemble, cluster, collect, congregate

The cousins <u>gather</u> together for a family picnic.

general *(adj)* common, normal, ordinary, typical, usual

Telephones have been in <u>general</u> use for almost one hundred years.

generate *(v)* create, make, originate, produce

Windmills can help <u>generate</u> electricity.

gentle *(adj)* kind, mild, softhearted, tender

My grandfather has a <u>gentle</u> manner.

get *(v)* acquire, gain, obtain, win

Do you <u>get</u> an allowance each week?

ghost *(n)* apparition, phantom, spirit, spook

Do you think a <u>ghost</u> haunts that old house?

gigantic *(adj)* colossal, enormous, huge, immense, tremendous

The Statue of Liberty is a <u>gigantic</u> monument.

give *(v)* deliver, dispense, furnish, provide, supply

<u>Give</u> me some water, please.

glad *(adj)* delighted, happy, joyful, joyous, pleased

The children were <u>glad</u> they had a snow day.

glance *(v)* glimpse, glint, peek, peep

Don't <u>glance</u> at the map while you are driving.

gloomy *(adj)* bleak, cheerless, dismal, dreary, somber

The clouds hid the moon and the stars on the <u>gloomy</u> night.

glory *(n)* grandeur, greatness, majesty, splendor

Do heroes always gain <u>glory</u> for their deeds?

go *(v)* depart, exit, leave, move, withdraw

<u>Go</u> home before it's too late.

good *(adj)* honest, honorable, noble, righteous, upright

Try your best to be a <u>good</u> citizen.

gorgeous *(adj)* attractive, beautiful, handsome, lovely, pretty

That floral bouquet is <u>gorgeous</u>.

gossip *(n)* buzz, hearsay, rumor, talk

Did you hear the <u>gossip</u> about the movie star?

govern *(v)* administer, administrate, direct, execute, oversee

Does a mayor _govern_ your town?

grab *(v)* grasp, nab, seize, snatch, take

Grab some tools and help build the tree house.

graceful *(adj)* effortless, flowing, smooth

The ballerina's performance was so _graceful_.

grade *(n)* degree, notch, rung, stage, step

What _grade_ are you in at school?

grain *(n)* bit, crumb, fragment, particle, speck

A _grain_ of sand is a tiny stone.

grand *(adj)* imposing, magnificent, majestic, stately

Doesn't that mansion look _grand_ behind its gates!

grateful *(adj)* appreciative, obliged, thankful

I'll be _grateful_ for your help.

graze *(v)* brush, flick, glance, shave, skim

Try to throw the stone so it will _graze_ the surface of the pond.

great *(adj)* distinguished, famous, notable, outstanding, prominent

Abraham Lincoln was a _great_ president.

greet *(v)* address, hail, salute, welcome

The friends _greet_ each other with a wave.

grieve *(v)* lament, mourn, sorrow, suffer

They will _grieve_ the loss of their dog.

grind *(v)* crush, mill, powder, pulverize

The millstones _grind_ wheat into flour.

grip *(v)* clasp, clutch, grasp, hold

Grip the rail on the steep staircase.

ground *(n)* dirt, earth, land, soil

Crops grow in the _ground_.

group *(n)* batch, bunch, clump, cluster, collection

A _group_ of lions is called a pride.

grow *(v)* age, develop, mature

Children get bigger as they _grow_.

growl *(v)* bellow, boom, grumble, roar, rumble

A bear will _growl_ when frightened.

guard *(v)* defend, protect, safeguard, secure, shield

The soldiers will _guard_ the fort.

guess *(v)* presume, reckon, suppose

Can you _guess_ the answer to the problem?

guide *(v)* conduct, direct, lead, pilot, steer

An explorer will _guide_ the pioneers across the prairie.

gummy *(adj)* gluey, gooey, sticky, tacky

The seat in the movie theater is _gummy_.

guy *(n)* chap, fellow, gentleman, man

Who is the _guy_ wearing the outrageous necktie?

h

habit *(n)* custom, manner, practice, way

Biting your fingernails is a bad _habit_.

hand *(n)* aid, assistance, help, relief

Give me a _hand_ with moving this heavy box.

handle *(v)* maneuver, manipulate, wield

The woodcutter can _handle_ the ax with ease.

handsome *(adj)* attractive, beautiful, fair, good-looking, lovely

Their son looks <u>handsome</u> all dressed up.

handy *(adj)* clever, expert, masterful, skillful

The carpenter is <u>handy</u> with tools.

hang *(v)* dangle, sling, suspend

<u>Hang</u> the birdfeeder from that branch.

happy *(adj)* delighted, glad, joyful, joyous, pleased

We're <u>happy</u> the long, cold winter is over.

hard *(adj)* compact, firm, solid

The pavement is <u>hard</u> compared to the grass.

harm *(v)* hurt, injure, wound

A poisonous snake can <u>harm</u> you.

haste *(n)* hurry, hustle, quickness, speed, swiftness

In my <u>haste</u> to catch the bus, I tripped on the sidewalk.

hatch *(v)* create, generate, make, originate, produce

An inventor likes to <u>hatch</u> new ideas.

hate *(v)* despise, detest, loathe

Don't you <u>hate</u> it when the bus is late?

haul *(v)* drag, lug, pull, tow, tug

Two horses will <u>haul</u> the cart.

head *(n)* boss, chief, director, leader, master

The president is the <u>head</u> of a company.

healthy *(adj)* fit, hearty, sound, strong, well

Eat well and exercise to stay <u>healthy</u>.

heap *(n)* accumulation, mass, mound, pile, stack

The dirty clothes were left in a <u>heap</u> on the floor.

hear *(v)* attend, hearken, heed, listen

Did you <u>hear</u> the crickets last night?

heat *(n)* hotness, warmness, warmth

The desert <u>heat</u> makes the air ripple.

heavy *(adj)* bulky, hefty, massive, weighty

That barbell is <u>heavy</u>.

help *(n)* aid, assistance, relief, support

Do you need <u>help</u> with your homework?

heroic *(adj)* brave, courageous, fearless, gallant, valiant

The <u>heroic</u> firefighter rescued the child from the burning building.

hesitate *(v)* falter, halt, pause, waver

I always <u>hesitate</u> when I get nervous during a speech.

hide *(v)* cloak, conceal, cover, screen, stash

Where did the squirrel <u>hide</u> its acorns?

hike *(n)* excursion, march, tramp, trek, walk

We took a long <u>hike</u> through the forest.

hire *(v)* employ, engage, retain

I hope this company will hire me for the job.

history *(n)* account, chronicle, narrative, report, story

We went to a museum to learn about the <u>history</u> of whaling.

hit *(v)* slam, smack, strike, swat, whack

The baseball player <u>hit</u> the ball into the outfield.

hold *(v)* clasp, clutch, grasp, grip

<u>Hold</u> on tight when you ride the roller coaster.

hole *(n)* cavity, crater, hollow, opening

The gopher dug a <u>hole</u> in the ground.

hollow

hollow *(adj)* empty, excavated, unfilled, vacant

The fox chased the rabbit into a hollow log.

home *(n)* abode, dwelling, habitation, residence

Our home is in an apartment building.

honest *(adj)* honorable, righteous, true, upright

Please give me your honest opinion.

honor *(n)* admiration, esteem, favor, regard, respect

The hero was held in the highest honor.

hop *(v)* bounce, jump, leap, spring, vault

The rabbits hop through the garden.

hopeful *(adj)* cheering, encouraging, likely, promising, reassuring

The patient wished for hopeful news from his doctor.

horrid *(adj)* awful, dreadful, ghastly, horrible, terrifying

Dracula was a horrid being.

horror *(n)* dread, fear, fright, panic, terror

The Halloween movie was full of horror.

hot *(adj)* blazing, burning, fiery, sizzling, steaming

Don't go too near the hot fire.

house *(n)* abode, dwelling, habitation, home, residence

Our family lives in a six-room house.

howl *(v)* bark, bay, wail, yowl

The wolves howl at the moon.

hug *(v)* clasp, embrace, squeeze

The toddler likes to hug his stuffed bunny around the neck.

immense

huge *(adj)* colossal, enormous, gigantic, immense, tremendous

The four-scoop sundae was huge.

human *(n)* individual, man, mortal, person, woman

The aliens had never seen a human before.

humor *(n)* comedy, funniness, wit

The circus clown has a great sense of humor.

hunt *(v)* chase, pursue, stalk, track, trail

Should people hunt animals for sport only?

hurry *(v)* dash, hasten, race, rush, scurry

You'll miss the bus if you don't hurry.

hurt *(v)* ache, burn, pain, smart, sting

Does it hurt where you cut your finger?

i

icy *(adj)* glassy, glazed, slick, slippery

The roads got icy when the temperature dropped.

idea *(n)* concept, impression, notion, perception, thought

A great idea just popped into my head.

ideal *(adj)* model, perfect, supreme

The sunny weather was ideal for a picnic.

ignore *(v)* disregard, neglect, snub

Don't ignore the car's warning signals.

imagine *(v)* conceive, envision, picture, see, visualize

Can you imagine life on another planet?

immense *(adj)* colossal, enormous, gigantic, huge, tremendous

Sculpting the presidents on Mount Rushmore was an immense project.

28

important

interruption

important (adj) meaningful, momentous, significant, substantial

Learning how to read is an important skill.

impossible (adj) impractical, unthinkable, unworkable

Traveling faster than the speed of light is impossible.

impress (v) affect, impact, influence, move, sway

Did the president's speech impress you?

improve (v) amend, better, help, upgrade

With your help we can improve the situation.

incident (n) episode, event, happening, occasion, occurrence

The principal will investigate the incident on the playground.

incorrect (adj) false, inaccurate, mistaken, untrue, wrong

The student had several incorrect answers on the test.

increase (v) amplify, enlarge, expand, extend, magnify

Will your parents increase your allowance?

indicate (v) mark, show, specify

The form will indicate where to fill in your name.

individual (n) being, creature, human, mortal, person

Many of our laws protect the rights of the individual.

industry (n) business, commerce, trade

The American automobile industry gets a lot of competition from abroad.

inform (v) advise, educate, enlighten, notify, tell

Inform me when you're ready to leave.

initial (adj) earliest, first, original, primary

I was nervous on my initial plane flight, but now I'm used to flying.

injure (v) damage, harm, hurt, wound

How did the athlete injure her knee?

innocent (adj) blameless, faultless, guiltless

In a court of law, you are innocent until proven guilty.

inquire (v) ask, examine, interrogate, question, quiz

Let's inquire at the gas station for directions.

inspect (v) check, examine, scrutinize, study, survey

Inspect the bananas for brown spots.

instruct (v) educate, teach, train, tutor

The teacher will instruct his students in math.

instrument (n) implement, tool, utensil

A pencil is a kind of writing instrument.

intelligent (adj) alert, bright, brilliant, clever, smart

Are you intelligent enough to figure out the puzzle?

intend (v) aim, design, mean, plan, propose

What do you intend to do with the lottery winnings?

interesting (adj) amusing, entertaining, exciting, fascinating, stimulating

Find an interesting book to read.

interfere (v) interrupt, intrude, meddle

A storm can interfere with TV reception.

interruption (n) break, disruption, pause, suspension

The fire drill provided an interruption from classes.

interval

knock

interval (n) breather, lull, pause, rest

There was a short interval between the basketball and baseball seasons.

invent (v) devise, compose, create, hatch, originate

Can the company invent a new product that everyone will want?

invite (v) ask, bid, call, request, summon

May I invite a friend over for dinner?

issue (v) circulate, dispatch, dispense, distribute

The store will issue a refund for returned merchandise.

j

jail (n) brig, lockup, penitentiary, prison

How many prisoners live in this jail?

jerk (v) lurch, tug, twitch, wrench, yank

A car out of gas may jerk to a stop.

job (n) assignment, chore, duty, task

It's my job to mow the lawn.

join (v) combine, connect, couple, link, unite

Let's join hands and make a circle.

joke (n) crack, gag, jest, quip, wisecrack

That joke had everyone laughing.

jolly (adj) festive, gay, gleeful, lighthearted, merry

Let's plan a jolly gathering to celebrate the company's twenty-fifth anniversary.

journey (n) excursion, expedition, tour, trek, trip

The travelers packed their bags for their journey.

joyful (adj) cheerful, gay, glad, happy, joyous

The baby made a joyful noise when she was raised into the air.

jump (v) bound, hurdle, leap, spring, vault

Kangaroos really know how to jump.

just (adj) appropriate, deserved, due, merited, rightful

The criminal got a just punishment from the jury.

k

keep (v) hold, reserve, retain, withhold

Where do you keep your belongings?

key (adj) chief, main, major, primary, principal

Who is the key witness in the criminal case?

kid (n) child, juvenile, youngster, youth

That kid looks like both of his parents.

kill (v) destroy, dispatch, eliminate, extinguish, finish

Some chemicals can kill plants in seconds.

kind (adj) compassionate, good, humane, kindhearted

The kind young man helped his neighbor carry her groceries upstairs.

kindle (v) fire, ignite, inflame, light

A spark can kindle a small fire.

king (n) lord, majesty, monarch, ruler

Is that country ruled by a king or queen?

knock (v) bang, pound, rap, tap, thump

Please knock on my door before entering my room.

knot

level

knot (v) bind, fasten, secure, tie

Knot your shoelaces so they don't come undone.

know (v) comprehend, fathom, grasp, understand

The teacher will give a test to see if his students know their math facts.

l

labor (n) grind, sweat, toil, work

Digging the ditch was hard labor.

lack (n) deficiency, insufficiency, scarceness, scarcity, shortage

The room was stuffy from the lack of fresh air.

land (n) dirt, earth, ground, soil

The farmer uses a plow to till the land.

language (n) dialect, jargon, lingo, speech, tongue

In this country, we speak the English language.

large (adj) big, enormous, gigantic, huge, immense

The bulldozer dug a large hole in the ground.

last (adj) closing, concluding, end, final, ultimate

Are you almost at the last page of the book?

late (adj) behind, belated, overdue, tardy

Hurry or you'll be late for your appointment.

latter (adj) following, later, subsequent, succeeding

The first half of the movie was not as exciting as the latter half.

laugh (v) chortle, chuckle, giggle, guffaw, snicker

The comedian hopes the audience will laugh at his jokes.

launch (v) propel, push, send, shove, thrust

NASA will launch the rocket into space tomorrow.

law (n) decree, ordinance, regulation, rule

Does your state have a law requiring the use of seat belts?

lead (v) conduct, direct, escort, guide, usher

The music teacher will lead the class in a song.

lean (v) incline, slant, slope, tilt, tip

What makes the fence lean to one side?

leap (v) bound, hurdle, jump, spring, vault

If you leap across the stream, you won't get wet.

learn (v) acquire, get, grasp, master

You can learn a lot by reading books.

leave (v) depart, exit, go, quit, withdraw

Please close the door behind you when you leave.

leisure (n) ease, relaxation, repose, rest

Weekends are a time for leisure.

lend (v) advance, credit, loan

Can you lend me some money to buy a comic book?

length (n) distance, extent, reach, span, stretch

The length of this ruler is one foot.

let (v) allow, grant, have, permit

Unlock the door and let me in.

level (adj) even, flat, flush, smooth

The carpenter used a plane to make the wood level.

liberty (n) freedom, independence, liberation

The colonists wanted <u>liberty</u> from their home country.

lift (v) boost, elevate, hoist, raise, uplift

Will you <u>lift</u> the chair so that I can sweep under it?

light (v) fire, ignite, inflame, kindle

Use matches to <u>light</u> the fire.

like (v) enjoy, relish, savor

I <u>like</u> to go to the beach on hot days.

limit (n) ceiling, extreme, limitation, maximum

Don't go faster than the speed <u>limit</u>.

limp (v) falter, halt, hobble, shuffle, stagger

After the operation on my leg, I might <u>limp</u> for a while.

line (n) file, queue, row, string, tier

A long <u>line</u> of people waited for movie tickets.

little (adj) miniature, minute, petite, small, tiny

The <u>little</u> toy car fit in the toddler's pocket.

live (v) abide, dwell, inhabit, occupy, reside

How many families <u>live</u> in that apartment building?

load (n) burden, cargo, freight, haul

The freight truck is carrying a heavy <u>load</u> of goods.

locate (v) discover, find, pinpoint, spot

Airports use radar to <u>locate</u> distant planes.

lone (adj) only, separate, single, sole, solitary

The <u>lone</u> wolf traveled across the tundra by itself.

look (v) observe, see, view, watch

<u>Look</u> carefully and you'll see the flaw.

loud (adj) blaring, deafening, noisy, piercing, roaring

The siren made a <u>loud</u> noise.

love (n) affection, attachment, bond, devotion, fondness

The children were always sure of their parents' <u>love</u>.

lovely (adj) attractive, beautiful, gorgeous, handsome, pretty

What a <u>lovely</u> dress you are wearing!

loyal (adj) faithful, resolute, staunch, steadfast, true

The singer's <u>loyal</u> fans go to all of her concerts.

lump (n) bulge, bump, knot, swelling

There's a <u>lump</u> on my arm where the bee stung me.

luster (n) glaze, gloss, polish, sheen, shine

The golden <u>luster</u> of the bracelet increased its beauty.

m

mad (adj) angry, enraged, furious, incensed, vexed

I'm <u>mad</u> at you for keeping me waiting.

magic (n) sorcery, witchcraft, wizardry

Can a wizard really perform <u>magic</u>?

magnificent (adj) grand, imposing, majestic, stately

A <u>magnificent</u> estate is perched on top of the hill.

mail (n) letters, messages, packages

Has the postal carrier brought today's <u>mail</u> yet?

major *(adj)* chief, key, main, primary, principal

Getting my car fixed is my <u>major</u> concern right now.

make *(v)* assemble, build, construct, manufacture, produce

Let's <u>make</u> a collage out of magazine clippings.

manage *(v)* conduct, direct, operate, run, supervise

The corporation hired a new employee to <u>manage</u> its sales department.

manner *(n)* bearing, behavior, presence, style, way

The butler had a very formal <u>manner</u>.

manufacture *(v)* assemble, build, construct, make, produce

Most companies <u>manufacture</u> their products in factories.

march *(v)* pace, step, stride, tread, walk

The band will <u>march</u> to the beat of the music.

margin *(n)* border, edge, fringe, perimeter, rim

The teacher wrote comments in the <u>margin</u> of my paper.

mark *(n)* indication, sign, symbol

Make a <u>mark</u> with your pencil next to each item you find on the scavenger hunt.

marvelous *(adj)* amazing, astonishing, fabulous, incredible, spectacular

The diver's triple back flip was <u>marvelous</u>!

mask *(v)* camouflage, cloak, conceal, disguise, hide

The embarrassed child tried to <u>mask</u> his feelings.

mass *(n)* accumulation, bulk, collection, quantity, volume

A great <u>mass</u> of storm clouds filled the sky.

master *(n)* authority, expert, pro, whiz, wizard

My sister is a <u>master</u> at the game of chess.

match *(n)* companion, double, duplicate, mate, twin

I can't find the <u>match</u> to this sock.

material *(n)* matter, stuff, substance

The expensive house was constructed with the best building <u>material</u>.

matter *(n)* affair, business, concern, situation

The committee will discuss the <u>matter</u> at its next meeting.

mean *(adj)* cruel, nasty, spiteful, vicious, wicked

Calling people names is a <u>mean</u> thing to do.

medal *(n)* badge, decoration, emblem, insignia, medallion

Who won a <u>medal</u> at the Olympics?

meet *(v)* confront, encounter, face, rendezvous

We'll <u>meet</u> later after school.

memorial *(n)* commemoration, monument, remembrance, reminder

The statue makes a fitting <u>memorial</u> to the dead hero.

memory *(n)* recall, recollection, remembrance

Do you have a good <u>memory</u> for phone numbers?

mend *(v)* fix, patch, repair, right

The tailor will <u>mend</u> the torn shirt with needle and thread.

mention *(v)* cite, name, specify

Did the principal <u>mention</u> which teachers would supervise the school dance?

33

merchant (n) businessperson, dealer, merchandiser, trader

The <u>merchant</u> sells goods in her store.

merry (adj) festive, gay, gleeful, jolly, lighthearted

The child felt <u>merry</u> after getting all her birthday presents.

mess (n) chaos, clutter, disorder, jumble

Clean up the <u>mess</u> in your room!

method (n) manner, system, technique, way

What is the best <u>method</u> for mining silver?

middle (n) center, core, midpoint, midst

Put a single candle in the <u>middle</u> of the cake.

might (n) brawn, muscle, power, strength, vigor

You'll need to use all of your <u>might</u> to move that couch.

mild (adj) compassionate, gentle, kind, soft, tender

The mother spoke to her baby in a <u>mild</u> voice.

mind (v) care, disapprove, object

Will your parents <u>mind</u> if we play loud music?

minor (adj) inconsiderable, insignificant, small, trivial, unimportant

The <u>minor</u> car trouble was quickly fixed at the gas station.

miserable (adj) forlorn, sad, sorrowful, woeful, wretched

I was <u>miserable</u> when I lost my concert tickets.

miss (v) crave, desire, need, want

I <u>miss</u> my friend who moved away.

mist (n) cloud, film, fog, haze, vapor

The early morning <u>mist</u> is making my hair damp.

mistake (n) blunder, error, miscue, slip

The student made a <u>mistake</u> on her homework.

mix (v) blend, combine, merge, mingle

The cook will <u>mix</u> the batter in a bowl.

modern (adj) contemporary, current, new, present-day, recent

Do you like old buildings or <u>modern</u> architecture?

moist (adj) damp, dank, dewy, wet

Her hair got curly in the <u>moist</u> air.

moment (n) flash, instant, minute, second, wink

The lightning flashed for a <u>moment</u>.

money (n) cash, currency, dollars, greenbacks, loot

Do you need <u>money</u> to buy groceries?

monster (n) beast, brute, demon, fiend, ghoul

The <u>monster</u> in this movie is really ugly.

mood (n) humor, spirit, temper

The boy whistles when he's in a good <u>mood</u>.

more (adj) added, additional, extra, fresh, further

You need <u>more</u> air to blow up the balloon completely.

motion (n) action, movement, stir, stirring

The train was already in <u>motion</u> when I reached the station.

mountain (n) alp, mount, peak

That <u>mountain</u> was once a volcano.

move (v) maneuver, remove, shift, transfer

Move your bicycle out of the driveway.

multiply (v) build, heighten, increase, mount, rise

Every year their household expenses multiply.

murder (n) homicide, killing, manslaughter, slaying

Have they found the weapon used to commit the murder?

muscle (n) brawn, might, power, strength, vigor

The movers used all of their muscle to move the piano.

mystery (n) puzzle, question, riddle

Do you enjoy the challenge of solving a mystery?

n

name (v) call, dub, entitle, term, title

What did the new parents name their child?

nap (n) catnap, doze, siesta, snooze

Are you tired enough to take a nap?

narrow (adj) close, confining, cramped, crowded, tight

Cars can pass only one direction at a time on the narrow bridge.

nation (n) commonwealth, country, land, republic, state

Our nation is bordered by ocean on two sides.

nature (n) character, disposition, makeup, personality, temperament

It's not my nature to hold a grudge.

naughty (adj) bad, ill-behaved, impish, misbehaving, mischievous

The naughty child put pepper in the salt shaker.

neat (adj) orderly, shipshape, spic-and-span, tidy, well-groomed

My room is always messy, and my brother's room is always neat.

necessary (adj) essential, imperative, important, required

It's necessary for rain to fall if plants are to grow.

need (v) lack, require, want

Does the soup need more salt to make it tasty?

neglect (v) disregard, fail, forget, ignore, overlook

Don't neglect to feed the dog, or he will start barking.

neighborhood (n) area, district, locality, vicinity

Our family is moving to a new neighborhood in town.

nerve (n) bravery, courage, fearlessness, spirit, spunk

Do you have the nerve to jump off the high diving board?

new (adj) creative, fresh, inventive, novel, original

The club members need to come up with a new idea for raising money.

news (n) advice, information, tidings, word

Have you heard news of the coming storm?

next (adv) after, afterward, later, subsequently

What television program is on next?

nice *(adj)* agreeable, good, pleasant, pleasing, pleasurable

How nice of you to bring me a snack!

nightfall *(n)* dusk, evening, sunset, twilight

Be home for dinner by nightfall.

noble *(adj)* admirable, good, honorable, moral, worthy

The rebel soldiers died fighting a noble cause.

noise *(n)* clamor, din, hubbub, racket, tumult

The fireworks make a lot of noise.

nonsense *(n)* craziness, folly, foolishness, silliness

This crazy story is a lot of nonsense.

normal *(adj)* common, general, ordinary, typical, usual

A normal day in July is quite hot.

nosy *(adj)* curious, inquisitive, prying, snoopy

The nosy neighbor was always peering out the window.

notice *(v)* distinguish, note, observe, see, view

Did you notice who walked in with mud on her boots?

notify *(v)* advise, inform, tell, warn

You must notify the fire department in case of fire.

now *(adv)* directly, immediately, instantly

Go clean your room right now.

nuisance *(n)* annoyance, bother, irritation

The raccoon that keeps getting into the trash can is a real nuisance.

o

obey *(v)* follow, heed, keep, mind, observe

The genie will obey your command.

object *(n)* article, device, item, gadget, thing

The fisher spotted an object bobbing in the water.

obtain *(v)* acquire, gain, get, win

Did you obtain the building permit so that we can begin construction?

occasion *(n)* episode, event, happening, incident, occurrence

The birthday party was a happy occasion.

occupation *(n)* employment, job, trade, vocation, work

What will your occupation be when you get a job?

occupy *(v)* inhabit, people, populate

How many families occupy that apartment building?

odd *(adj)* curious, peculiar, queer, strange, weird

It was an odd feeling visiting my former home.

offend *(v)* insult, outrage, slight

Rude behavior can offend a lot of people.

offense *(n)* aggression, assault, attack, strike

The football team's strong offense scored four touchdowns.

offer *(v)* extend, give, present

The book club will offer a free gift to new members.

officer *(n)* administrator, director, executive, manager, official

My mother is an officer of a bank.

pain

old (adj) aged, ancient, antique

That old book is ready to fall apart.

omit (v) delete, drop, eliminate, exclude, remove

If you omit an ingredient from the recipe, the food may taste odd.

open (v) unbar, unblock, unclose, unlock, unshut

Here's the key to open the door.

operate (v) handle, run, use, work

Do you know how to operate a fax machine?

opinion (n) belief, conviction, feeling, sentiment, view

Your opinion is not based on fact.

oppose (v) challenge, dispute, fight, resist

If you oppose my views, we will disagree.

orbit (v) circle, circuit, cycle, round

The satellite will orbit the planet.

order (n) arrangement, distribution, formation, grouping, sequence

Put the books in their proper order on the shelf.

ordinary (adj) average, common, plain, unexceptional, unremarkable

An ordinary stone is not valuable.

organize (v) arrange, classify, group, order, sort

When will you organize your desk drawers?

original (adj) earliest, first, initial, primary

The original painting has brighter colors than the copy.

outfit (n) costume, dress, getup, guise

What a stunning outfit you're wearing!

outline (n) draft, rough, skeleton, sketch

I made an outline of my report before I wrote it.

outstanding (adj) excellent, exceptional, magnificent, superb, terrific

The speaker's outstanding presentation had everyone clapping.

overcome (v) beat, conquer, defeat, overpower, subdue

Most immigrants had to overcome serious problems in their new homeland.

overflow (v) drown, engulf, flood, submerge, swamp

Did the heavy rains overflow the basement?

overturn (v) overthrow, topple, upset

Did the playful dog overturn the vase and break it?

owed (adj) due, outstanding, payable, unpaid, unsettled

Is that bill still owed or did you pay it?

own (v) have, hold, possess, retain

Do you own the book or did you borrow it?

p

pace (n) gait, quickness, rapidity, speed, swiftness

The walker was moving at a quick pace.

pack (v) fill, heap, load, pile

How many books can you pack into that box?

pageant (n) ceremony, display, parade, show, spectacle

The school put on a pageant about Thanksgiving.

pain (n) ache, hurt, pang, soreness, stitch

After running two miles, I felt a pain in my side.

paint (n) coloring, dye, pigment, stain, tint

We used watercolor paint to make pictures in art class.

pair (n) couple, duo, twosome

I need a new pair of sneakers.

pale (adj) colorless, doughy, ghostly, wan

His skin was very pale when he was sick.

papa (n) dad, daddy, father, pa, pop

Those two people are my mama and papa.

paper (n) article, composition, essay, report, theme

The student is writing a paper on the dangers of smoking.

parcel (n) lot, plot, tract

This parcel of land will have a house built on it.

part (n) division, piece, portion, section, segment

What part of the movie did you like best?

particular (adj) individual, special, specific

What particular food is your favorite?

partner (n) ally, associate, colleague, comrade, mate

My mother is looking for a business partner to help her manage her company.

party (n) affair, celebration, festivity, function, occasion

All of my friends came to my birthday party.

pass (v) advance, go, journey, proceed, travel

Will you pass through your grandparent's birthplace on your trip abroad?

patch (v) fix, mend, repair, right

The bicyclist had to patch a flat bike tire.

pause (v) falter, halt, hesitate, waver

Don't pause too often during your speech.

peaceful (adj) calm, placid, restful, serene, tranquil

The campers enjoyed the peaceful setting in the mountains.

peculiar (adj) bizarre, odd, strange, unusual, weird

The refrigerator had a peculiar smell coming from it.

peek (v) glance, glimpse, glint, peep

Don't peek while I find a place to hide.

perform (v) act, do, portray, represent

I hope to perform in the school talent show.

perfume (n) aroma, fragrance, scent

Some kinds of perfume smell like flowers.

period (n) age, days, era, time

What period in history are you studying now?

permit (v) allow, authorize, let, sanction

Does the school permit students to wear hats in class?

persuade (v) assure, convince, satisfy

I'll try to persuade the coach to let me play in the next game.

phrase (v) express, formulate, put, word

Politicians are careful about how they phrase their remarks.

physical (adj) concrete, material, real, substantial, tangible

The detectives need physical evidence to solve the crime.

pick (v) choose, handpick, select, take

Carefully pick out apples at the supermarket.

picture

popular

picture (n) depiction, drawing, illustration, portrayal, representation

There was a picture of an octopus in the encyclopedia.

piece (n) division, part, portion, section, segment

There is one piece of pie left on the plate.

pierce (v) cut, gash, slash, slice, slit

Did the thorn pierce your skin?

pile (n) accumulation, heap, mass, mound, stack

We raked up a pile of leaves in the yard.

pin (v) affix, attach, fasten, fix, secure

Pin the name tag to your shirt.

pit (n) core, kernel, nut, seed, stone

There's a pit in the middle of a peach.

pitch (v) cast, hurl, sling, throw, toss

The baseball player will pitch a fast ball.

pity (n) charity, compassion, mercy, sympathy

Everyone felt pity for the hurricane victims.

place (n) location, point, position, site, spot

There's one place in the backyard where grass won't grow.

plain (adj) apparent, clear, distinct, evident, obvious

The answer to the question was plain to me.

plan (v) aim, design, intend, mean, propose

What do you plan to do on this rainy afternoon?

plant (n) factory, mill, shop, works

It always smells good near the chocolate plant.

play (n) diversion, fun, recreation, sport

Recess is a time for play.

pleasant (adj) agreeable, enjoyable, nice, pleasing, pleasurable

Paddling a canoe is a pleasant way to spend time.

pledge (v) promise, swear, vow

We pledge allegiance to the flag.

point (n) dot, pinpoint, speck, spot

There was one point on the map I couldn't name.

poke (v) dig, jab, nudge, prod, punch

If I fall asleep during the lecture, poke me with your elbow.

police (n) cop, law, patrol, officer

The police direct traffic during rush hour.

policy (n) course, line, plan, procedure, program

What is the school's policy regarding homework?

polish (v) buff, glaze, gloss, rub, shine

I must polish my scuffed shoes.

polite (adj) civil, courteous, mannerly, respectful, well-mannered

It is polite to say "please" and "thank you."

pollute (v) contaminate, dirty, foul, poison

The fumes from the factory smokestack will pollute the air.

poor (adj) broke, needy, penniless, poverty-stricken, strapped

The poor man was homeless.

pop (v) bang, boom, burst, crack, explode

The cork on the bottle will pop when opened.

popular (adj) favored, favorite, preferred, well-liked

The shy teenager wished he were more popular.

portion (n) lot, part, ration, share

My portion of pizza is smaller than yours.

position (n) location, place, site, situation, spot

The ticket buyer changed her position in line.

positive (adj) assured, certain, confident, sure

The coach was positive his team would win the championship.

possess (v) have, hold, own, retain

I possess a collection of baseball cards.

post (n) appointment, position, situation, station

The new ambassador began her post in a foreign country.

pound (v) batter, beat, hammer, hit, pelt

Use a mallet to pound the stake into the ground.

power (n) authority, command, control, mastery, might

The president has more power in government than any other person.

practical (adj) functional, handy, useful

Learning to sew is a practical skill.

practice (v) drill, exercise, rehearse

The football players practice their plays all afternoon.

praise (v) applaud, commend, compliment, hail

Teachers praise students who try their best.

preacher (n) clergyman, clergywoman, minister, parson, reverend

The preacher gave a sermon on Sunday.

precious (adj) costly, invaluable, priceless, valuable, worthy

Diamonds are a kind of precious stone.

prepare (v) fit, fix, make, ready

What will you prepare for dinner?

present (adj) contemporary, current, existing, immediate, latest

The lawn mower is not working in its present condition.

pressure (n) strain, stress, tension

The surgeon felt a lot of pressure in the operating room.

pretend (v) act, fake, feign, make believe

Some nights I pretend to be asleep when I'm not.

pretty (adj) attractive, beautiful, good-look

What pretty wild flowers are growing in the meadow!

prevail (v) best, conquer, master, overcome, triumph

We hope for good to prevail over evil.

prevent (v) block, hamper, hinder, obstruct, stop

We put up a tall fence to prevent our dog from getting out of the yard.

previous (adj) former, past, preceding, prior

Turn back to the previous page in your book.

price (n) charge, cost, expense

The price of the airline tickets went up today.

principal (adj) chief, key, main, major, primary

The Constitution contains the principal laws of the United States.

prison (n) brig, jail, lockup, penitentiary

The convicted criminals were sent to prison.

prize (n) award, premium, reward

The student won a prize for writing the best story.

40

probability *(n)* chance, likelihood, odds, possibility, prospect

There is a high probability that it will rain in April.

problem *(n)* difficulty, dilemma, plight, predicament

The youngster was having a problem with a bully on the playground.

procedure *(n)* approach, course, plan, tack, technique

Open-heart surgery is a complicated procedure.

proceed *(v)* go, journey, pass, travel

We will proceed cautiously on the icy road.

produce *(v)* create, generate, make, originate

Composers produce original songs.

program *(n)* agenda, calendar, schedule, timetable

The program for today's meeting includes three speakers.

progress *(v)* advance, come, march, move, proceed

Was the project able to progress without a leader?

promise *(v)* pledge, swear, vow

Promise you'll be back before dark.

pronounce *(v)* say, utter, vocalize, voice

The judge will pronounce the sentence for the criminal.

proper *(adj)* appropriate, apt, fitting, right, suitable

The guests must wear proper clothes to a formal wedding.

propose *(v)* offer, pose, present, submit, suggest

Did you propose any ideas during the conference?

prosper *(v)* boom, flourish, succeed, thrive

The store will prosper if it attracts enough customers.

protect *(v)* defend, guard, safeguard, secure, shield

Wear sun block to protect your skin from burning.

proud *(adj)* arrogant, disdainful, haughty, lordly, superior

The man was too proud to admit his mistakes.

provide *(v)* deliver, dispense, furnish, give, supply

Our garden will provide all the vegetables we need.

public *(n)* community, people, society

The city park is open to the public.

pull *(v)* drag, draw, haul, tow, tug

The tugboats pull the ocean liners into the harbor.

purchase *(v)* acquire, buy, get, obtain, shop

At which store did you purchase your shirt?

pure *(adj)* absolute, perfect, plain, sheer, unmixed

Pure gold is too soft for most kinds of jewelry

purpose *(n)* aim, design, goal, intent, intention, plan

The purpose of this meeting is to devise a plan.

pursue *(v)* chase, follow, hunt, seek, trail

The police will pursue the escaped prisoners.

push *(v)* drive, propel, shove, thrust

Push hard to open the sticky door.

put *(v)* fix, lay, place, set

Put the forks on the left side of the plate.

q

qualified *(adj)* able, capable, competent, skilled

An astronaut is qualified to fly in a spacecraft.

quality *(n)* characteristic, feature, mark, property, trait

Look at the excellent quality of the craftsmanship.

quantity *(n)* amount, body, bulk, measure, total

Fishing nets catch fish in vast quantity.

quarter *(n)* area, district, neighborhood, region, zone

The lights went out in our quarter of the town.

queer *(adj)* curious, odd, peculiar, strange, weird

Seeing my look-alike gave me a queer feeling.

question *(v)* ask, examine, inquire, interrogate, quiz

The lawyer will question the witness during the trial.

quick *(adj)* fast, rapid, speedy, swift

A cheetah is a quick animal.

quiet *(adj)* hushed, noiseless, silent, soundless, still

The class was quiet while taking a test.

quit *(v)* cease, discontinue, halt, stop

When are you going to quit biting your nails?

quite *(adv)* completely, entirely, fully, totally, wholly

I believe you are quite right about that issue.

r

race *(n)* competition, contest, rivalry

The tortoise won the race against the hare.

radiate *(v)* beam, blaze, gleam, glow, shine

The stars radiate light.

ragged *(adj)* frayed, shredded, tattered, worn

Throw out that ragged shirt.

raid *(v)* assail, assault, attack, charge, storm

The soldiers will raid the enemy's fort.

raise *(v)* boost, elevate, hoist, lift, uplift

Use a forklift to raise the load of goods from the warehouse floor.

range *(n)* extent, orbit, reach, scope, sweep

The rocket has a range of a thousand miles.

rank *(n)* place, position, standing, station, status

A colonel has a higher rank than a captain.

rapid *(adj)* fast, quick, speedy, swift

The musical group made a rapid rise to fame.

rare *(adj)* exceptional, extraordinary, remarkable, uncommon, unusual

That rare plant grows only in the rain forest.

real *(adj)* authentic, genuine, original, true

Real lemonade is made with fresh lemons.

reason *(n)* excuse, explanation, justification

Do you have a good reason for being late?

receive *(v)* accept, admit, get, obtain, take

Did you receive a lot of birthday cards in the mail?

reckless *(adj)* brash, hasty, impulsive, rash

The prisoner made a <u>reckless</u> dash for freedom.

recognize *(v)* detect, distinguish, identify, know

My friends didn't <u>recognize</u> me with my new haircut.

recommend *(v)* advise, counsel, suggest

Ask the librarian to <u>recommend</u> a good book.

recover *(v)* reclaim, regain, repossess, retrieve

The police hope to <u>recover</u> all of the stolen property.

reduce *(v)* decrease, diminish, dwindle, lessen

You can <u>reduce</u> your weight by eating well and exercising.

refuse *(v)* decline, dismiss, reject, spurn

I always <u>refuse</u> my friend's suggestion to go skydiving.

regard *(v)* admire, esteem, honor, respect, value

The museum visitors <u>regard</u> the painting with awe.

region *(n)* area, district, section, territory, zone

The river flooded the whole <u>region</u> around it.

regret *(n)* anguish, grief, heartache, sadness, sorrow

She felt deep <u>regret</u> at hurting her friend's feelings.

regular *(adj)* common, normal, routine, typical, usual

Our family goes hiking on a <u>regular</u> basis.

reign *(v)* govern, rule, sway

The king and queen <u>reign</u> over their country.

release *(v)* discharge, free, liberate

The hijackers will <u>release</u> all of the airplane passengers.

relief *(n)* aid, assistance, help, support

The Red Cross provided <u>relief</u> after the earthquake.

remain *(v)* linger, stay, tarry, wait

I will <u>remain</u> in class after the bell rings to speak to my teacher.

remark *(n)* comment, note, observation

The critic made a nasty <u>remark</u> about the actor's performance.

remember *(v)* recall, recollect, retain, revive

<u>Remember</u> that sleepover when we had a pillow fight?

repair *(v)* fix, mend, patch, right

Can the mechanic <u>repair</u> the car?

reply *(n)* answer, response, retort

I wrote to my favorite actress and am waiting for a <u>reply</u>.

report *(n)* account, chronicle, history, narrative, story

The teacher asked us to write a <u>report</u> about our summer vacation.

represent *(v)* illustrate, mirror, symbolize, typify

Circled stars <u>represent</u> state capitals on the map.

require *(v)* ask, demand, involve, necessitate, take

Does the toy <u>require</u> batteries to run?

reserve *(v)* hold, keep, retain, withhold

I <u>reserve</u> the right to change my mind.

resist *(v)* combat, fight, oppose, repel, withstand

How long can the small army <u>resist</u> the mighty enemy?

respect (v) admire, esteem, honor, regard, value

I _respect_ people who stand up for their beliefs.

respond (v) answer, reply, retort

The guest speaker will _respond_ to questions after her speech.

rest (n) ease, leisure, relaxation, repose

The tired boy took a long _rest_ in the hammock.

result (n) consequence, effect, outcome

Lava poured down the side of the volcano as a _result_ of the eruption.

retreat (v) depart, evacuate, recoil, retire, withdraw

The battered troops were forced to _retreat_.

rich (adj) moneyed, prosperous, wealthy, well-off, well-to-do

We will be _rich_ if we win the lottery.

right (adj) accurate, correct, exact, precise, proper

Is there a _right_ way to eat with chopsticks?

rise (v) arise, ascend, lift, mount, soar

Watch the smoke _rise_ into the air.

risk (n) danger, hazard, peril

There is always some _risk_ in parachuting.

road (n) avenue, boulevard, drive, street, way

Construction trucks blocked traffic on the _road_.

roam (v) drift, meander, ramble, rove, wander

Do you want to _roam_ down the beach with me?

roar (v) bellow, cry, howl, shout, yell

Listen to the football fans _roar_ with excitement.

rod (n) bar, shaft, stick

Hang the drapes on a curtain _rod_.

rot (v) decay, disintegrate, spoil, turn

The fruit will _rot_ in the sun.

rough (adj) coarse, craggy, jagged, rugged, uneven

Use _rough_ sandpaper to smooth out the bumpy spots on the table.

rude (adj) discourteous, disrespectful, ill-mannered, impolite, ungracious

The _rude_ audience booed during the play.

ruin (v) demolish, destroy, destruct, smash, wreck

The incoming waves will _ruin_ the sand castle.

rule (v) govern, reign, sway

Kings _rule_ over their kingdoms.

run (v) dash, scamper, scoot, scurry, sprint

We had to _run_ to catch the bus.

rush (v) dash, hurry, race, scurry, speed

If you _rush_, you'll catch the train.

S

sad (adj) dejected, depressed, downcast, melancholy, unhappy

The _sad_ child cried quietly in his room.

safe (adj) protected, secure, sheltered, shielded

The rabbit found a _safe_ place to hide from the fox.

sailor (n) mariner, navigator, seafarer

How many months was the _sailor_ at sea?

salary (n) earnings, fee, pay, wages

The employee's _salary_ increased by 5 percent.

salute (v) address, greet, hail

The soldiers must <u>salute</u> any officer who passes by.

satisfy (v) appease, content, fulfill, gratify, please

Will a large sandwich <u>satisfy</u> your appetite?

savage (adj) ferocious, fierce, untamed, vicious, wild

A lion is a <u>savage</u> beast.

save (v) deliver, free, liberate, rescue

Rescuers were able to <u>save</u> the climbers trapped on the mountaintop.

say (v) communicate, convey, declare, express, state

The lecturer had much to <u>say</u> in her speech.

scale (v) ascend, climb, mount

The climbers used special equipment to <u>scale</u> the mountain.

scarce (adj) infrequent, rare, sparse, uncommon

Two-dollar bills are <u>scarce</u> these days.

scare (v) alarm, frighten, spook, startle, terrify

Do spiders <u>scare</u> you?

scatter (v) disperse, distribute, spread, sprinkle, strew

The organizers of the treasure hunt will <u>scatter</u> clues in all directions.

scene (n) outlook, perspective, sight, view, vista

The artist is painting an ocean <u>scene</u>.

scent (n) aroma, odor, smell

Do you like the <u>scent</u> of fresh lemons?

scold (v) chide, reprimand, reproach

The pet owner must <u>scold</u> the naughty puppy.

score (n) count, number, sum, tally, total

Which soccer team had the higher <u>score</u>?

scowl (n) frown, glare, glower, grimace

The angry coach wore a <u>scowl</u> on his face.

scrap (n) bit, fragment, particle, shred, speck

Pick up that <u>scrap</u> of paper on the floor.

scrape (v) rub, scour, scrub

Use a sponge to <u>scrape</u> the food off the plate.

scream (v) screech, shriek, shrill, squeal

Some people <u>scream</u> when riding a roller coaster.

screen (v) cover, protect, shelter, shield

Put netting over the carriage to <u>screen</u> the baby from mosquitoes.

search (v) hunt, quest, seek

Will you help me <u>search</u> for my missing keys?

seat (n) base, capital, center, headquarters

Washington, D.C., is the <u>seat</u> of our federal government.

second (n) flash, instant, moment, twinkle, wink

Wait here; I'll be back in a <u>second</u>.

secure (adj) defended, protected, safe, sheltered

Hide your valuables in a <u>secure</u> place in the house.

see (v) distinguish, note, notice, observe, view

How well could they <u>see</u> the stage from their seats in the back row?

seek (v) hunt, pursue, quest, search

It's my turn to hide and your turn to <u>seek</u>.

45

seize *(v)* clutch, grab, nab, snatch

I will seize the rope as it swings by.

select *(v)* choose, pick, prefer, take

What flavor of juice did you select from the vending machine?

sell *(v)* market, peddle, trade

Every Saturday merchants sell wares at an outdoor market.

send *(v)* dispatch, forward, route, ship, transmit

Please send the package by overnight delivery.

sentimental *(adj)* emotional, gushy, romantic, syrupy

The poet wrote a sentimental love poem.

separate *(adj)* apart, detached, independent, individual, unconnected

My sister and I have separate rooms.

serious *(adj)* earnest, grave, sober, solemn, somber

The boy wore a serious expression as he studied.

set *(v)* fix, lay, place, put, settle

Set the grocery bags on the kitchen counter.

severe *(adj)* brutal, extreme, hard, harsh, rough

The warm spring gladdened us after suffering a severe winter.

shake *(v)* quake, quiver, shiver, shudder, tremble

Sometimes when I'm nervous, my hands shake.

shame *(n)* discredit, disgrace, dishonor

The youths' crime brought shame to their families.

shape *(v)* form, model, mold

The baker will shape the dough into a loaf of bread.

share *(v)* dispense, distribute, divide, parcel, portion

Will you share your colored markers with me?

sharp *(adj)* alert, bright, clever, intelligent, smart

The scholar has a sharp mind.

shed *(v)* cast, emit, project, radiate

The moon will shed some light in the yard.

shelter *(n)* cover, haven, protection, refuge

During the thunderstorm, the hikers found shelter in a cave.

shine *(v)* beam, blaze, gleam, glow, radiate

Shine the flashlight on the path ahead.

ship *(v)* dispatch, forward, route, send, transmit

The foreign manufacturer will ship its product to the United States by freighter.

shock *(v)* jar, jolt, shake, startle, stun

Do horror tales easily shock you?

shoot *(v)* discharge, fire, hurtle, project, propel

How many people can shoot a basketball from center court into the hoop?

shout *(v)* bellow, cry, holler, roar, yell

From this distance, no one will hear you unless you shout.

shove *(v)* drive, propel, push, thrust

A few pushy people tried to shove their way to the front of the crowd.

shovel *(v)* dig, excavate, scoop

You must shovel the snow on the sidewalk.

show *(v)* demonstrate, display, exhibit, illustrate

Show us how to make pizza.

shut *(v)* bolt, close, fasten, latch, lock

I made sure I had my keys before I shut the door.

sigh *(n)* breath, mumble, murmur, whisper

The contestant let out a sigh after winning the first round.

sign *(n)* evidence, indication, mark, stamp, token

Having a black cat cross your path is supposed to be a sign of bad luck.

silent *(adj)* hushed, noiseless, quiet, soundless, still

The busy neighborhood was silent late at night.

silly *(adj)* absurd, crazy, foolish, ridiculous, wacky

People laugh at the silly saying on my T-shirt.

similar *(adj)* alike, comparable, corresponding, equivalent, like

My best friend and I have similar interests.

simple *(adj)* easy, effortless, smooth, straightforward

Boiling an egg is a simple task.

sincere *(adj)* genuine, honest, real, true

Our family is making a sincere effort to recycle.

single *(adj)* lone, sole, unattached, unmarried, unwed

My single aunt announced that she is getting married.

sink *(v)* descend, drop, fall

The servants must sink to their knees when they greet the emperor.

situation *(n)* case, circumstances, condition, plight, predicament

How will lawmakers deal with the crime situation in this country?

sketch *(n)* design, diagram, draft, drawing, rough

The artist drew a sketch of the scene before she painted it.

skid *(v)* slide, slip, slither

Cars might skid on the icy road.

skill *(n)* ability, command, knack, mastery

The youths practiced a lot to develop their skill at skateboarding.

skim *(v)* browse, glance, riffle, scan

The reader had time only to skim the newspaper.

slam *(v)* bang, clap, crash, whack

Don't slam the door shut!

slice *(v)* cut, gash, pierce, slash, slit

Be careful that you don't slice your finger on that sharp piece of metal.

slip *(v)* skid, slide, slither

Watch your step, or you will slip on the ice.

slow *(adj)* deliberate, leisurely, poky, sluggish, unhurried

The slow turtle plodded along the beach.

small *(adj)* little, miniature, minute, petite, tiny

The small mouse squeezed through the hole in the wall.

smart *(adj)* alert, bright, clever, intelligent, sharp

Wearing a helmet when riding your bike is a smart thing to do.

smash *(v)* break, fracture, shatter, splinter

It is the custom to smash a bottle against the bow of a new ship.

smell (n) aroma, odor, scent

Don't you just love the <u>smell</u> of home-baked bread!

smile (v) beam, grin, laugh

The photographer tried to get the anxious child to <u>smile</u>.

smooth (adj) even, flat, flush, level

The new bike path has a <u>smooth</u> surface.

snap (v) break, fracture, split

Twigs <u>snap</u> easily.

sneak (v) creep, glide, lurk, prowl, slink

Can we <u>sneak</u> into the house and hide the present without being noticed?

snoop (v) mouse, nose, poke, pry

My little sister is not allowed to <u>snoop</u> in my room.

sob (v) bawl, blubber, cry, wail, weep

The movie was so sad, it made me <u>sob</u>.

soft (adj) mushy, spongy, squashy, squishy, yielding

Do you like a <u>soft</u> pillow for sleeping?

soiled (adj) dirty, filthy, grimy, grubby, unclean

Put the <u>soiled</u> laundry into the washing machine.

sole (adj) lone, only, separate, single, solitary

Is Earth the <u>sole</u> planet with life forms?

solid (adj) compact, firm, hard

The water in the pail froze into <u>solid</u> ice.

solution (n) answer, discovery, result

Can you find a <u>solution</u> to the problem?

solve (v) decipher, explain, resolve, unravel

Use a calculator to <u>solve</u> the math problems.

sore (adj) aching, hurting, painful, smarting

The dog limped on his <u>sore</u> leg.

sorrow (n) anguish, grief, heartache, regret, sadness

The nation felt <u>sorrow</u> over the leader's death.

sort (v) assort, categorize, classify, group, separate

The novelist will <u>sort</u> her notes and then begin writing her first draft.

source (n) beginning, origin, root, spring, well

Has the plumber found the <u>source</u> of the leak?

space (n) distance, expanse, reach, spread, stretch

Measure the <u>space</u> between the two walls.

speak (v) chatter, communicate, converse, talk

The two friends <u>speak</u> on the phone every day.

special (adj) individual, particular, specific

Most sports require a <u>special</u> kind of footwear.

specimen (n) case, example, illustration, instance, sample

The biologist looked at the <u>specimen</u> under a microscope.

speed (n) pace, quickness, rapidity, swiftness

The state trooper clocked the car's <u>speed</u> at 70 miles per hour.

spin (v) swirl, twirl, whirl

If you <u>spin</u> in circles too long, you'll get dizzy.

spirit (n) animation, life, liveliness, vigor, vitality

The students were full of <u>spirit</u> at the football rally.

splendid (adj) glorious, sensational, superb, terrific, wonderful

Our family had a <u>splendid</u> time at the fair.

split *(n)* break, chink, cleft, crack

That plank of wood has a <u>split</u> in it.

spoil *(v)* decay, rot, turn

Put the meat into the refrigerator so that it will not <u>spoil</u>.

spooky *(adj)* eerie, scary, weird, uncanny

Walking in the dark cave gave us a <u>spooky</u> feeling.

spot *(n)* blemish, blot, mark, stain

There's a <u>spot</u> of ketchup on his white shirt.

spread *(v)* expand, extend, open, unfold

<u>Spread</u> your napkin and put it on your lap.

spring *(v)* bound, hurdle, jump, leap, vault

Watch the track star <u>spring</u> over those hurdles!

stack *(v)* heap, lump, mound, pile

<u>Stack</u> the test papers neatly on my desk.

stake *(v)* bet, gamble, wager

The investors were willing to <u>stake</u> a lot of money on the success of the new business.

stalk *(v)* chase, hunt, pursue, track, trail

On TV, we watched a tiger <u>stalk</u> its prey.

standard *(adj)* basic, customary, normal, regular, routine

What is the <u>standard</u> price for a car wash?

stare *(v)* eye, gape, gaze, glare, look

It's not polite to <u>stare</u> at people.

start *(v)* begin, commence, initiate, launch, undertake

We will <u>start</u> a new chapter in our history book.

startle *(v)* jolt, shock, surprise

Did I <u>startle</u> you when I tapped you on the shoulder?

state *(n)* condition, situation, status

What is the patient's current <u>state</u>?

stay *(v)* linger, remain, tarry, wait

Please <u>stay</u> and have dinner with us.

steal *(v)* pinch, rob, snatch, thieve

What did the thieves <u>steal</u> from the store?

step *(v)* pace, stride, tread, walk

Remove your shoes before you <u>step</u> across the wet floor.

sticky *(adj)* humid, muggy, soggy, sultry

The <u>sticky</u> weather made everyone uncomfortable.

stiff *(adj)* inflexible, rigid, unbending, unyielding

The soldier marches with a <u>stiff</u> back.

still *(adj)* immobile, motionless, stationary, unmoving

The active child had difficulty sitting <u>still</u>.

sting *(v)* bite, burn, hurt, smart

Chlorine in a pool can make your eyes <u>sting</u>.

stir *(v)* blend, combine, merge, mingle, mix

<u>Stir</u> the pancake batter until it's smooth.

stop *(v)* cease, discontinue, halt, quit

All traffic must <u>stop</u> at a red light.

story *(n)* fable, fiction, narrative, tale, yarn

Every night her father reads her a <u>story</u> at bedtime.

strain *(n)* pressure, stress, tension

The car-repair bill put a <u>strain</u> on their budget.

strange *(adj)* bizarre, odd, peculiar, unusual, weird

What is that <u>strange</u> object flying in the sky?

stray *(v)* meander, ramble, roam, rove, wander

Would your cat ever <u>stray</u> far from home?

strength (n) brawn, might, muscle, power, vigor

The swimmer has tremendous <u>strength</u> in her arms.

stretch (v) extend, lengthen, prolong

After sitting all day, I wouldn't wait to <u>stretch</u> my legs.

strike (v) hit, slam, smack, swat, whack

<u>Strike</u> the gong with the padded mallet.

stroll (v) amble, meander, ramble, saunter, walk

Many people <u>stroll</u> through the park on weekends.

strong (adj) brawny, mighty, powerful

The <u>strong</u> workhorse pulled the plow.

stubborn (adj) hardheaded, obstinate, pigheaded, tough, unyielding

The <u>stubborn</u> child refused to eat his vegetables.

study (v) consider, contemplate, ponder, weigh

Scientists <u>study</u> the effect of pollution on human health.

stupid (adj) dense, dim-witted, dull, dumb, slow

Locking myself out was a <u>stupid</u> thing to do.

subject (n) matter, point, text, theme, topic

What is the <u>subject</u> of the article you're reading?

substance (n) material, matter, stuff

The toy was made of a plastic <u>substance</u>.

substitute (v) change, exchange, swap, switch, trade

In this recipe, you can <u>substitute</u> honey for sugar.

succeed (v) flourish, prosper, thrive

How many restaurants <u>succeed</u> in their first year?

sudden (adj) abrupt, hasty, headlong, hurried

A driver honked at me for making a <u>sudden</u> turn.

suffer (v) bear, endure, sustain, tolerate, undergo

Did you <u>suffer</u> much pain when you broke your toe?

sufficient (adj) adequate, decent, enough, satisfactory

Allow <u>sufficient</u> time to get to the busy airport.

suggest (v) offer, pose, propose, submit

Hairdressers often <u>suggest</u> new hairstyles to their customers.

supply (v) deliver, dispense, furnish, give, provide

The youth group will <u>supply</u> canned goods to the food drive.

support (v) bolster, brace, carry, sustain, uphold

Can those thin columns <u>support</u> the weight of the porch roof?

suppose (v) assume, guess, presume, reckon

Which candidate do you <u>suppose</u> will win the election?

surprise (v) amaze, astonish, astound, flabbergast, startle

Let's <u>surprise</u> Mom and Dad by cleaning our room without being asked.

surrender (v) abandon, cede, resign, waive, yield

Good parents never <u>surrender</u> their authority.

surround (v) circle, encircle, enclose, ring

Several onlookers <u>surround</u> the street performer.

survey (v) examine, inspect, overlook, scrutinize, study

The president will visit the disaster site to survey the damage.

swamp (n) bog, marsh, wetland

Do alligators live in that swamp?

sway (v) rock, swing, wave

The tree branches sway in the wind.

sweet (adj) sugary, sweetened, syrupy

The chocolate dessert was too sweet.

swift (adj) fast, quick, rapid, speedy

A bullet train is a swift passenger train.

switch (v) change, exchange, substitute, swap, trade

I will switch this sweater for one in a bigger size.

sympathy (n) compassion, concern, pity

The girl felt sympathy for the hungry dog and gave it a biscuit.

t

take (v) accept, gain, get, obtain, receive

Please take some tomatoes from our garden.

tale (n) fable, fiction, narrative, story, yarn

Have you ever read a tale about a flying ship?

talk (v) chat, communicate, converse, speak

Talk softly in the movie theater.

tall (adj) high, lofty, soaring, towering

Skyscrapers are tall buildings.

tame (adj) gentle, meek, mild

Our dog is a tame animal.

tasty (adj) appetizing, delicious, mouth-watering, savory

This restaurant serves tasty food.

tax (n) assessment, duty, levy, tariff

I paid a sales tax on the CDs I bought.

teach (v) educate, instruct, school, train, tutor

Can you teach me to play tennis?

tear (v) cleave, rip, split

I will tear my messy paper in two and start again.

tease (v) annoy, harass, pester, plague, worry

Sometimes kids tease me about my height.

tell (v) communicate, convey, declare, express, state

Can I tell you a secret?

temperate (adj) moderate, modest, reasonable

San Diego has a temperate winter climate.

tend (v) attend, mind, watch

Will you tend the fire while we put up the tent?

term (n) duration, span, stretch, time

Senators serve a term of six years.

terrible (adj) appalling, awful, dreadful, horrible, shocking

There was a terrible car accident on the highway.

territory (n) area, district, region, section, zone

Our sales force covers the northeast territory.

terror (n) dread, fear, fright, horror, panic

The monster movie gripped us with terror.

test (n) exam, examination, quiz

We will have a spelling test on Friday.

51

thankful *(adj)* appreciative, grateful, obliged

Be thankful that the mechanic could repair your car problem right away.

theory *(n)* assumption, guess, premise

A theory is an idea that is often hard to prove.

thick *(adj)* broad, bulky, fat, solid, wide

Cut thick slices from the loaf of bread.

thin *(adj)* lean, skinny, slender, slight, slim

If you lose any more weight, you'll be too thin.

thing *(n)* article, item, object

What is that thing in the box?

think *(v)* conceive, imagine, picture, see, visualize

Do you think you would like being famous?

though *(conj)* although, whereas, while

It's hot today, though not as hot as yesterday.

thoughtful *(adj)* attentive, considerate, courteous, kind, polite

It was thoughtful of you to bring me a drink.

thrill *(v)* delight, electrify, enthuse, excite

The rodeo riders thrill the audience with their daring acts.

through *(adj)* completed, concluded, done, ended, finished

Tell me when you are through with your chores.

throw *(v)* cast, hurt, pitch, sling, toss

The quarterback will throw the football down the field.

thunder *(n)* bang, blast, boom, burst, roar

The fierce storm provided fifteen minutes of thunder and lightning.

ticket *(n)* label, marker, tag

Read the ticket to find out how much the jacket costs.

tie *(v)* bind, fasten, knot, secure

Tie your shoelaces tightly.

tight *(adj)* close, confining, cramped, crowded, narrow

Can we all fit into that tight space?

timid *(adj)* bashful, modest, retiring, shrinking, shy

The child was too timid to speak to grown-ups.

tinker *(v)* fiddle, fidget, play, putter, trifle

My dad likes to tinker with gadgets in his workshop.

tiny *(adj)* dwarf, miniature, minute, small, teeny

The stars look like tiny lights in the night sky.

tip *(n)* advice, clue, hint, pointer, suggestion

Here's a tip on how to save energy.

tire *(v)* drain, exhaust, fatigue, weary

Did the ten-mile walk tire you?

tool *(n)* implement, instrument, utensil

A pocketknife is a useful camping tool.

top *(n)* crest, crown, peak, summit

The top of the mountain is always covered with snow.

toss *(v)* heave, pitch, roll

The big waves toss the small rowboat.

touch *(v)* feel, finger, handle

Touch how soft and smooth the velvet is.

tough *(adj)* hardy, stout, strong, sturdy

A cactus is a tough plant that needs little water.

tour *(v)* circle, circuit, cycle, orbit, round

This summer we will tour the countryside on our bikes.

52

uncertain

track (v) follow, shadow, tail, trace, trail

The hunters will <u>track</u> the deer's footprints in the snow.

trade (v) change, exchange, substitute, swap, switch

Do you want to <u>trade</u> your apple for my orange?

train (v) educate, instruct, school, teach, tutor

The company will <u>train</u> its employees on how to use the new computer equipment.

transport (v) bear, carry, convey, haul, lug

The ship will <u>transport</u> goods overseas.

trap (n) bait, decoy, lure, snare, temptation

The criminal fell into the lawyer's <u>trap</u> and was caught lying.

travel (v) go, journey, pass, proceed

How many states will you <u>travel</u> through on your car trip?

treasure (n) fortune, riches, wealth, worth

The divers searched for <u>treasure</u> in the sunken ship.

tremendous (adj) colossal, enormous, gigantic, huge, immense

Tyrannosaurus rex was a <u>tremendous</u> dinosaur.

trick (v) deceive, dupe, fool, mislead

Will the sly fox <u>trick</u> the foolish crow?

trim (v) clip, crop, pare, prune, shave

The barber will <u>trim</u> the man's shaggy hair.

trip (n) excursion, journey, tour, travel, voyage

Would you like to take a <u>trip</u> around the world?

triumph (n) conquest, victory, win

The team members will celebrate their <u>triumph</u> over last year's champions.

trouble (v) alarm, concern, distress, upset, worry

Would seeing a snake <u>trouble</u> you?

true (adj) faithful, loyal, resolute, staunch, steadfast

A <u>true</u> friend can be trusted.

trust (n) belief, confidence, faith, reliance

I have the deepest <u>trust</u> in my friend's loyalty.

try (v) attempt, endeavor, strive, struggle, undertake

You must <u>try</u> to control your temper.

turn (v) circle, revolve, rotate

<u>Turn</u> the spinning wheel round and round.

twilight (n) dusk, evening, nightfall, sunset

The streetlights go on at <u>twilight</u>.

twin (n) companion, double, duplicate, match, mate

Help me find the <u>twin</u> to this glove.

twist (v) coil, curl, spiral, wind

<u>Twist</u> the string around the top.

type (n) breed, class, kind, sort, variety

What <u>type</u> of spiders are poisonous?

U

ugly (adj) hideous, homely, plain, unattractive

The rhinoceros is an <u>ugly</u> animal.

unable (adj) incapable, incompetent, powerless, unfit, unqualified

The inexperienced magician was <u>unable</u> to pull a rabbit out of his hat.

uncertain (adj) doubtful, dubious, skeptical, undecided, unsure

The injured athlete was <u>uncertain</u> she could compete in the upcoming game.

uncomfortable *(adj)* awkward, nervous, tense, uneasy

There was an <u>uncomfortable</u> silence when the actor forgot his lines.

uncommon *(adj)* infrequent, occasional, rare, scarce, seldom

It is <u>uncommon</u> to see a shooting star.

understand *(v)* comprehend, fathom, grasp, know

I <u>understand</u> the concept now that you've explained it.

uneasy *(adj)* edgy, fidgety, jittery, jumpy, nervous

I felt <u>uneasy</u> entering the dark house.

unfortunate *(adj)* luckless, misfortunate, unlucky

The <u>unfortunate</u> family, lost their home to the flood.

unhappy *(adj)* dejected, depressed, downcast, melancholy, sad

Are you <u>unhappy</u> because your birthday is over?

uniform *(adj)* alike, comparable, corresponding, equivalent, similar

Every item coming off the assembly line had a <u>uniform</u> quality.

union *(n)* alliance, association, confederation, league, society

The <u>union</u> of American colonies became the United States.

unite *(v)* combine, connect, couple, join, link

We must <u>unite</u> in our quest for world peace.

unjust *(adj)* one-sided, unbalanced, unequal, unfair

The harsh punishment was <u>unjust</u>.

unnecessary *(adj)* needless, nonessential, unneeded, unrequired

It was <u>unnecessary</u> to wear a sweatshirt on such a hot day.

unpleasant *(adj)* bad, disagreeable, displeasing, offensive

The week-old garbage had an <u>unpleasant</u> smell.

unusual *(adj)* exceptional, extraordinary, rare, remarkable, uncommon

This zoo contains some <u>unusual</u> animals.

urge *(v)* press, prod, prompt, propel, spur

I <u>urge</u> you to try out for the soccer team.

use *(v)* apply, employ, exercise, implement, utilize

<u>Use</u> a whisk to beat the eggs.

usher *(v)* conduct, direct, escort, guide, lead

At the theater, someone will <u>usher</u> you to your seat.

usual *(adj)* common, normal, ordinary, regular, typical

The highway was backed up with the <u>usual</u> morning traffic.

utter *(v)* articulate, express, say, vocalize, voice

Don't <u>utter</u> a sound.

V

vacant *(adj)* bare, empty, stark, void

The <u>vacant</u> building was run-down.

vacation *(n)* break, holiday, leave, rest

We visited our grandparents during our <u>vacation</u>.

vain *(adj)* fruitless, futile, ineffective, unsuccessful, useless

We made a <u>vain</u> attempt to keep the waves from destroying our sand castle.

valuable *(v)* costly, invaluable, precious, priceless, worthy

The safe was filled with valuable jewels.

vanish *(v)* clear, disappear, evaporate, fade

That stain will vanish after you wash the shirt.

vary *(v)* alter, change, convert, modify

Sometimes I like to vary my route home.

vast *(adj)* enormous, extensive, huge, immense, tremendous

Antarctica is covered by a vast sheet of ice.

venture *(n)* adventure, enterprise, exploit, feat

Exploring in the jungle can be a dangerous venture.

very *(adv)* exceptionally, extremely, greatly, highly, remarkably

The ocean is very deep.

vicinity *(n)* area, district, locality, neighborhood

During the storm, lightning struck in our vicinity.

victory *(n)* conquest, triumph, win

The baseball game ended in a victory for our team.

view *(n)* outlook, perspective, scene, sight, vista

Our view of the Grand Canyon was spectacular.

visible *(adj)* seeable, viewable, visual

The sun is barely visible behind the clouds.

vulgar *(adj)* coarse, crude, rough, rude, uncivilized

It is vulgar to spit in public.

W

wait *(v)* linger, remain, stay, tarry

Wait for me to go with you.

wake *(v)* awake, awaken, rouse, stir

Set the alarm clock to wake me in the morning.

walk *(v)* amble, promenade, ramble, saunter, stroll

Hundreds of shoppers walk through the mall.

wander *(v)* drift, meander, ramble, roam, rove

The tourists wander through the streets of Paris.

want *(v)* crave, desire, need, require, wish

Do you want anything to eat?

war *(n)* conflict, fighting, strife, warfare

The war started with a fierce battle.

ward *(v)* avert, avoid, fend, prevent

Keeping clean can help ward off disease.

warm *(adj)* compassionate, kindhearted, responsive, sympathetic, tender

The doctor has a warm manner with her patients.

warn *(v)* alarm, alert, caution, forewarn

The alarm will warn us if burglars break in.

wash *(v)* clean, cleanse, launder

Wash your hands with soap and water.

waste *(n)* debris, garbage, refuse, rubbish, trash

All of the waste is overflowing the trash barrel.

watch *(v)* look, observe, regard, scrutinize, see

Watch that plane do skywriting.

way (n) manner, method, mode, system, technique

The magician has a special <u>way</u> of making coins disappear.

weak (adj) delicate, feeble, fragile, frail

The hospital patient felt <u>weak</u> after the operation.

wealth (n) assets, fortune, money, riches, worth

The millionaire donates part of his <u>wealth</u> to charity.

weary (adj) exhausted, fatigued, tired, wearied, worn-out

The runner was <u>weary</u> after finishing the marathon.

weighty (adj) bulky, heavy, hefty, massive

A crane lifted the <u>weighty</u> steel beams.

weird (adj) eerie, spooky, supernatural, uncanny, unearthly

Do you hear a <u>weird</u> noise coming from the attic?

welcome (v) greet, hail, salute

The crowd will <u>welcome</u> the governor when she arrives.

well (adj) fit, healthy, hearty, sound, strong

The patient was feeling <u>well</u> enough to walk around.

wet (adj) drenched, soaked, sodden, soggy, sopping

Did you get <u>wet</u> in the downpour?

while (n) bit, space, spell, stretch, time

I haven't seen you in a <u>while</u>.

whimper (v) cry, sniffle, sob, weep, whine

We heard the dog <u>whimper</u> in pain after it ran into the thorny bush.

whip (v) beat, lash, strike, thrash

The stagecoach driver will <u>whip</u> the horses to make them run faster.

whisper (v) mumble, murmur, mutter

The baby is taking a nap, so please <u>whisper</u>.

whiz (v) dash, race, speed, zip, zoom

The skaters <u>whiz</u> past me on their roller blades.

whole (adj) all, complete, entire, total

Will you eat the <u>whole</u> sundae by yourself?

wide (adj) ample, roomy, spacious

The couch is so <u>wide</u> that four people can sit on it.

wiggle (v) squiggle, squirm, worm, wriggle, writhe

The worms <u>wiggle</u> in the dirt after the rain.

wild (adj) native, natural, uncultivated

In the summer, <u>wild</u> blueberries grow along the roadside.

win (v) beat, overcome, prevail, triumph

Can we <u>win</u> the Ping-Pong tournament?

wind (n) air, breeze, gust

The strong <u>wind</u> blew down the road sign.

wind (v) coil, curl, spiral, twine, twist

<u>Wind</u> the string up into a ball.

wise (adj) intelligent, knowing, knowledgeable, sage

Owls are thought to be <u>wise</u> birds.

wish (v) crave, desire, want

What did you <u>wish</u> for on your birthday?

witness (n) eyewitness, observer, onlooker, spectator, viewer

Were you a <u>witness</u> to the accident?

wolf (v) gobble, gulp, guzzle

Don't <u>wolf</u> down your food.

wonder (n) marvel, miracle, phenomenon, sensation

The northern lights are a <u>wonder</u> of the sky.

word (n) comment, remark, statement, utterance

When I argue with my older brother, he always has to have the last word.

work (v) grind, labor, sweat, toil

The gardener must work hard pulling up weeds.

worm (v) crawl, creep, slide, snake

Can you worm through the space under the fence?

worry (v) ail, concern, distress, trouble, upset

Many matters worry the president.

worsen (v) decline, degenerate, descend, disintegrate, sink

The patient's condition will worsen if the new medicine doesn't work.

worth (n) account, valuation, value

What is the estimated worth of the ruby necklace?

wound (v) damage, harm, hurt, injure

Did the enemy soldiers wound anyone during the battle?

wrap (v) cloak, enfold, envelop, shroud, veil

The clouds wrap the moon like a blanket.

wrench (v) wrest, wring, wry

The big sailfish could wrench the fishing rod out of my hand.

wrestle (v) grapple, scuffle, tussle

I wrestle other students in my weight group.

write (v) author, compose, create, pen, produce

Will the movie star write a novel based on her life?

wrong (adj) false, inaccurate, incorrect, mistaken, untrue

Did you have any wrong answers on the test?

y

yard (n) court, courtyard, enclosure

In the fall, we rake leaves in the yard.

yell (v) bellow, cry, holler, roar, shout

You don't have to yell; I can hear you.

yes (adv) absolutely, agreed, all right, aye, OK

Yes, I'd like to go to the movies with you.

yet (adv) eventually, finally, someday, sometime, ultimately

This brain teaser is difficult, but I'll solve it yet.

yield (v) abandon, forsake, relinquish, surrender

The citizens refuse to yield their right to free speech.

youth (n) adolescent, juvenile, minor, teen, teenager

The youth turns sixteen years old today.

z

zero (n) naught, nil, nothing, zilch

The score is five to zero.

zip (v) fly, race, speed, whiz, zoom

The race cars zip around the speedway.

zone (n) area, district, quarter, region, territory

Can a business succeed in the zone of the town?

zoom (v) fly, race, speed, whiz, zip

See the skiers zoom down the mountain slope!

Additional words and their synonyms

Additional words and their synonyms

Additional words and their synonyms

Additional words and their synonyms

Additional words and their synonyms

Additional words and their synonyms

Additional words and their synonyms